PEARL OF GREAT PRICE

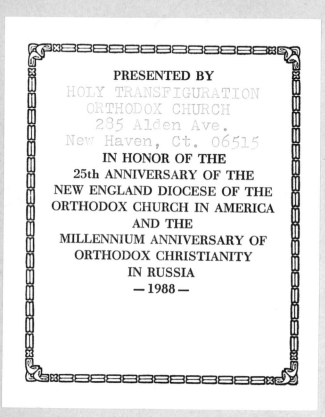

PEARL OF GREAT PRICE

The Life of Mother Maria Skobtsova
1891–1945

SERGEI HACKEL

Foreword by
Metropolitan Anthony of Sourozh

Darton, Longman & Todd
London

St Vladimir's Seminary Press
Crestwood, New York 10707
1981

First published in Great Britain in 1965
by Darton, Longman & Todd Ltd
under the title *One, of Great Price*

This revised edition published in Great Britain in 1982 by
Darton, Longman & Todd Ltd
89 Lillie Road, London SW6 1UD

Published in 1982 in the U.S.A. by
St Vladimir's Seminary Press
575 Scarsdale Road
Crestwood, New York 10707

ISBN 0 232 51540 9 (DLT)
ISBN 0-913836-85-0 (SVS Press)

British Library Cataloguing in Publication Data

Hackel, Sergei
[One of great price]. Pearl of great price.
1. Skobtsova, Maria   2. Russkaia pravoslavnaia
'tserkov'—Biography
I. Title   II. Pearl of great price
281.9′092′4   BX597.S/

ISBN 0–232–51540–9

Library of Congress Cataloging in Publication Data

Hackel, Sergei.
  Pearl of great price.

  Rev. ed. of: One of great price. London: Darton,
Longman & Todd, 1965; and based on Mat' Mariia, 1980.
  Bibliography: p.
  Includes index.
  1. Mariia, Mother, 1891–1945.   2. Nuns—France—
Biography.   3. World War, 1939–1945—Prisoners and
prisons, German.   I. Title.
BX597.M3H32   1981   281.9′3 [B]   81-21356
ISBN 0–913836–85–0   AACR2

Typeset by Input Typesetting, London SW19 8DR
Printed in Great Britain by The Anchor Press Ltd
and bound by Wm Brendon & Son Ltd
both of Tiptree, Essex

The kingdom of heaven
is like unto a merchant man,
seeking goodly pearls:
who, when he had found
one pearl of great price,
went and sold all that he had,
and bought it.

Matthew 13:45–6

CONTENTS

Acknowledgements   viii

List of Illustrations   ix

Foreword by Metropolitan Anthony of Sourozh   xi

Bibliographical Note   xiii

Abbreviations   xiv

1 Deprivation   1

2 A Straitening of the Way   9

3 Monasticism   20

4 The House at Rue de Lourmel   28

5 Orthodox Action   50

6 The Second Commandment   69

7 Forebodings   75

8 War   98

9 Martyrdom   123

Bibliography   150

Index   155

ACKNOWLEDGEMENTS

It is pleasant to recall that this work was originally undertaken with the encouragement of Mother Maria's own mother, Sophia Borisovna Pilenko (1862–1962). I could hardly have proceeded with the original version without the friendship and co-operation of Mother Elizaveta Medvedeva and Fedor Timofeevich Pianov. Igor' Aleksandrovich Krivoshein first urged and constantly supported the preparation of the Russian text. I would like to record my gratitude to them, as well as to other individuals who provided information, advice and support over the years. My gratitude is extended both to those whose assistance is recorded in my footnotes and to those whose contribution was in some way less specific. I am indebted to Hazel Ireson for generous and expert secretarial support. Greg Hackel gave valuable advice on the illustrations and provided some of them. At all times I have gained immeasurably from the sensitivity and critical acumen of my wife, as well as from her love.

S.H.

ILLUSTRATIONS

(between pages 48 and 49)

1 *Childhood*. Liza Pilenko aged eleven (1903).
2 *Motherhood*. Elizaveta Kuz'mina-Karavaeva with Gaiana and her nursemaid, together with her mother and her brother (*c.* 1915).
3 *Exile*. Elizaveta Skobtsova with her children Iura, Nastia and Gaiana (1923).
4 *Bereavement*. Nastia Skobtsova in hospital, drawn by her mother (1926).
   (Photo: University of Sussex MSU.)
5 *Episcopal support*. Metropolitan Evlogii Georgievskii (1929).
6 *Theological debate*. At a conference of the Russian Student Christian Movement (1934).
7 *Service of the needy*. 77 rue de Lourmel (1965).

(between pages 112 and 113)

8 *Monasticism 'in the world'*. Mother Maria in the yard at Lourmel (1937).
9 *Monasticism 'in the world'*. Mother Maria with Mother Evdokia and Mother Liubov' (mid 1930s).
10 *Lay support*. Fedor Timofeevich Pianov (late 1930s).
11 *Poetry*. The first draft of a poem by Mother Maria, followed by a fair copy (*c.* 1933).
   (Photo: Greg Hackel.)
12 *Isolation*. A self-portrait by Mother Maria (*c.* 1937).
13 *Parish life*. A new priest arrives at Lourmel (1939).

ix

14 *Parish priest*. Fr Dimitrii Klepinin (1939).
15 *Embroidery*. Mother Maria at her work (early 1940s).
    (Photo: Greg Hackel.)
16 *Supreme sacrifice*. Central figures of the Last Supper embroidery (1940–1).
    (Photo: University of Sussex MSU.)
17 *Victory over evil*. An embroidery worked by Mother Maria in Ravensbrück concentration camp (1944).
    (Photo by courtesy of Rosane Lascroux.)

FOREWORD BY METROPOLITAN ANTHONY OF SOUROZH

Mother Maria is remembered in the context of the Russian Emigration, the French Resistance or Ravensbrück concentration camp. But her achievement extends beyond the circumstances of her life, and it outlives them. For above all, by way of her Christian dedication and in her own distinctive style, she demonstrated what it means to be human.

In the process she sacrificed her personal serenity. Since her life was completely interwoven with the destiny of her contemporaries, their turmoil was hers, their tragedy was hers. And yet she was not swept away by it. She was anchored in God and her feet rested on the Rock.

Infinite pity and compassion possessed her; there was no suffering to which she was a stranger; there were no difficulties which could cause her to turn aside. She could not tolerate hypocrisy, cruelty or injustice. The Spirit of Truth which dwelt in her led her to criticize sharply all that is deficient, all that is dead in Christianity and, particularly, in what she mistakenly conceived to be classical monasticism. Mistakenly, for what she was attacking was an empty shell, a petrified form. At the same time, with the perception of a seer, she saw the hidden, glorious content of the monastic life in the fulfilment of the gospel, in the realization of divine love, a love which has room to be active and creative in and through people who have turned away from all things and – above all – from themselves in order to live God's life and to be his presence among men, his compassion, his love. 'God so loved the world, that he gave his only begotten Son, that whosoever believeth in him should not perish, but have everlasting life': this she understood, this she lived for. This is also what she died for.

Mother Maria is a saint of our day and for our day: a woman of flesh and blood possessed by the love of God, who stood fearlessly face to face with the problems of this century.

May this impressive book encourage its readers to emulate her merciless criticism of all hypocrisy and to follow their own path with equal courage. May they find in her inspiration to live as she lived, to accept death as she did.

ANTHONY
Metropolitan
of Sourozh

BIBLIOGRAPHICAL NOTE

Something like fifteen years have passed since the first version of this book appeared.[1] This was soon to be followed by a German edition.[2] The latter gave birth to a documentary film for German television (1968), in the preparation for which I was able to review the already familiar documentation as well as to consult previously unknown or inaccessible sources. Over the years various secondary works have appeared, several of which were published in the USSR. More important, a Mother Maria archive was assembled by Mother Elizaveta Medvedeva (1890–1974) and Fedor Timofeevich Pianov (1889–1969), which was eventually to pass into my care. All this seemed to necessitate as well as to facilitate the expansion and revision of the original work.

Ultimately it was the appearance in Moscow of a *samizdat* translation of my book which prompted me to return to the text and to prepare a new Russian version for publication in Paris (1980).[3] It was this which was to provide the basis for the present work, although it is not identical with it. But both these recent versions supersede the original of 1965.

---

[1] *One, of Great Price. The Life of Mother Maria Skobtsova, Martyr of Ravensbrück.* Darton, Longman and Todd, 1965.
[2] *Die grössere Liebe. Der Weg der Maria Skobcova (1891–1945).* Düsseldorf, Patmos Verlag, 1967; an excellent translation by Annemarie Böll (the wife of Heinrich Böll).
[3] *Mat' Mariia (1891–1945).* Paris, YMCA-Press, 1980.

ABBREVIATIONS

Evlogii	*Put' moei zhizni. Vospominaniia Mitropolita Evlogiia.* Izlozhennye po ego razskazam T. Manukhinoi. Paris 1947.
Hackel, *One, of Great Price* (1965)	Sergei Hackel, *One, of Great Price. The Life of Mother Maria Skobtsova, Martyr of Ravensbrück.* London 1965.
Hackel, *MM* (1980)	Sergii Gakkel' [=Hackel], *Mat' Mariia (1891–1945).* Paris 1980.
Manukhina	T. Manukhina, 'Monakhinia Mariia', *Novyi zhurnal*, vol. 41 (1955), pp. 137–57.
Memoir	The term refers to a wide range of documents, most of them short, many of them unpublished. In almost all cases they contain first-hand reminiscences of Mother Maria.
MM (1947)	*Mat' Mariia: stikhotvoreniia, poemy, misterii, vospominaniia ob areste i lagere v Ravensbriuke.* Paris 1947.
MMP	Mother Maria Papers. A variety of papers, including MSS of Mother Maria's poems, MSS and typescripts of her articles (published and unpublished), correspondence, reminiscences by various hands; also graphic and photographic material. Deposited with the author.
Mochul'skii	K. Mochul'skii, 'Monakhinia Mariia Skobtsova', *Tretii Chas*, No. 1 (1946), pp. 64–73.
o.	Oral communication. Statements of 1964 were tape-recorded for broadcasting. Others are based on detailed notes made in the course of interviews.
Pravoslavnoe Delo (1939)	*Pravoslavnoe Delo. Sbornik I.* Paris 1939.

Ruf' (1916)	E. Kuz'mina-Karavaeva, *Ruf'*. Petrograd 1916.
Stikhi (1937)	Monakhinia Mariia, *Stikhi*. Berlin [1937].
Stikhi (1949)	Mat' Mariia, *Stikhi*. Paris 1949.
Tillion, *Ravensbrück* (1973)	Germaine Tillion, *Ravensbrück*. Paris 1973
TsGALI	*Tsentral'nyi Gosudarstvennyi arkhiv literatury i iskusstva*. Moscow.
VRDP	*Vestnik Russkikh Dobrovol'tsev, Partizan i Uchastnikov Soprotivleniia vo Frantsii*, No. 1 (1946), No. 2 (1947) [no more published].
'Vstrechi s Blokom'	E.Iu. Kuz'mina-Karavaeva, 'Vstrechi s Blokom. (K piatnadtsatiletiiu so dnia smerti)'. *Uchenye zapiski Tartuskogo gosudarstvennogo universiteta*, vyp. 209 (1968), pp. 267–78. Introduction by D. E. Maksimov, pp. 257–64.

TRANSLITERATION OF RUSSIAN

I have used a simplified form of the Library of Congress system. Exceptions are made for a number of common names, such as Evdokia, Evgenia, Maria, Sophia. The rendering of the surname Pianov (=P'ianov) is rendered less cumbersome by the omission of the soft sign.

1

DEPRIVATION

Revolution and civil war uprooted more than a million Russians in the years 1917–22 and brought them into exile.[1] Europe was still licking her own war wounds and was not in the best position to receive them. It was fortunate they had no intention of staying for long: for a season, at most for a year, only until the end of Bolshevik rule. They were not alone in the delusion, shared by many a government, that the spectre of Communism was but a fleeting apparition.

As the months lengthened into years it became increasingly evident that the exiles were not likely to return home even within a generation. In the capitals of Europe – Berlin, Belgrade, Prague, Sofia and Paris foremost among them – Russian schools and churches, publications, foods and entertainments became part of the accepted scene.[2] To be driven by a Russian taxi driver to a Parisian theatre at which Russian drama, opera or ballet was being presented by an émigré Russian company was nothing out of the ordinary in the 1920s, and there was many a Russian restaurant or night club at which the evening might be rounded off. It needed the Russian beggar at the night club doors to remind the public that it was none the less an alien world in which the exiles lived, a world in which they formed what a League of Nations report called 'a social group *sui generis*, least favoured in the fight for existence'. For the ballerinas, impresarios and

[1] Some early estimates spoke of nearly two million Russians in Europe alone. In addition there was an emigration to the Far East (more than 130,000 refugees). On the statistics see J. H. Simpson, *The Refugee Problem* (London 1939), pp. 62–116.

[2] See the handbooks published by V. Konorov, *Spravochnik russkikh uchrezhdenii, lits i torgovo-promyshlennykh predpriiatii v Parizhe* (Paris 1921); and *Spravochnik russkikh uchrezhdenii [. . .] za granitsei* (Paris 1922).

restauranteurs were only one part of the scene: 'in the harsh fight for survival, the majority of émigrés, no matter what their social position at home, were obliged to descend to the lowest possible rungs of the social ladder.'[3]

Early in 1923 a family of such émigrés arrived in Paris. Its arrival caused no stir and it was recorded only by immigration officials. The family consisted of six: Elizaveta (to her familiars, Liza) Skobtsova; her mother, Sophia Pilenko; her second husband, Daniil Skobtsov; her son Iura and her two daughters. Gaiana, the eldest of the children, had been born in Russia when her mother's first marriage was already passing beyond estrangement to divorce. The youngest, Nastia, had been born in the newly-formed Kingdom of the Serbs, Croats and Slovenes on the eve of her family's move to France.

They had come the way of many others. From the eastern shores of the Black Sea (Novorossiisk) they had travelled south to the then independent Menshevik republic of Georgia (Tblisi), eventually westwards to Constantinople, then on to Belgrade. Some of the journey was uneventful, some dangerous and degrading; all was comfortless, an unsought-for progression from home towards no certain substitute for one.

The most difficult stage of the journey was the first. A mass evacuation was under way at Novorossiisk as the civil war in the Kuban region drew to a close in March 1920. The steamer on which Liza Skobtsova had managed to gain a place was one of the last available. Inevitably it was packed to capacity. None the less commercial considerations determined the distribution of passengers. First and second class passengers crowded the upper decks. Below them was a layer of Armenian refugees. Next, a deck reserved for sheep. Less profitable passengers were confined to the hold. Here it was pitch dark, but no naked lights were allowed: the retreating White troops had brought a cargo of explosives with them in the vain hope that the war might not have ended yet. A further reminder of the war was provided by the wounded. Their fellow-passengers in the hold feared to stumble over them in the dark-

[3] V. V. Rudnev, *Usloviia zhizni detei v emigratsii* (Paris 1928), p. 3.

ness and restricted their own movements as much as they could.

A pregnant Liza travelled in this hold together with her mother and her as yet only child, both dependent on her. For the civil war had also separated her from her husband during that first year of their marriage. No doubt his absence weighed on her mind. But her principal concern was to avoid the premature birth of his child in the dismal turmoil of the hold. Nothing in her subsequent travels during the difficult years 1920–3 could compare with the brutality of this introduction to her life as refugee.

In the event Iura was to be born safely on the outskirts of Tblisi in April 1920. A few months later his parents were to be reunited in Constantinople, where they found congenial lodgings for a while. But Constantinople was in no state to meet any long-term demands made by several hundred thousand Russian refugees, least of all in the last days of its ill-fated sultanate. With the help of the newly devised 'Nansen passports' (1922) the Skobtsovs journeyed on.[4]

Their arrival in France solved no economic problems. Liza permanently damaged her short-sighted eyes by sewing, making dolls, designing stencils for silk scarves. Even together with her husband's earnings as a part-time teacher and his token pension from the Kuban government in exile, the family's daily income barely rose to fifteen francs per day. The situation was somewhat eased when Skobtsov qualified as a taxi driver and thus ensured a more regular and more generous daily income of forty to fifty francs. But the family's financial problems were to be completely overshadowed by the infant Nastia's ill health.

The parents were slow to realize that she was seriously ill. It seemed reasonable to suppose that she was merely suffering from the after-effects of the influenza which had affected all the family during the hard winter of 1925–6. But even in this undernourished family it was Nastia's constant loss of weight which began to cause alarm, the more so when none of the

---

[4] On the Nansen passport see J. H. Simpson, *The Refugee Problem* (London 1939), pp. 239–42, 266–8.

doctors consulted could offer a diagnosis or suggest effective countermeasures. Her condition was already critical when a new young doctor on his first visit correctly diagnosed tuberculous meningitis.

Nastia was immediately admitted to the Pasteur Institute. Thanks to the intervention of Mechnikov's widow, Liza was given permission to stay at Nastia's side. For the greater part of two long months she was to witness her daughter's decline. A record of her watch is provided by six pastel portraits of Nastia which she sketched to afford each of them some relief. They depict the frail features of an unduly calm and clearly feverish child. Three of the sketches are dated at various hours of 7 March 1926. It was to be the day of Nastia's death.[5]

Nastia's death was to have unexpected and permanent repercussions in the life of her mother. A note which Liza scribbled at the time already gives an indication of them:

> For years I did not know, in fact I never knew the meaning of repentance, but now I am aghast at my own insignificance[. . .]. At Nastia's side I feel that my soul has meandered down back alleys all my life. And now I want an authentic and a purified road, not out of faith in life, but in order to justify, understand and accept death[. . .]. No amount of thought will ever result in any greater formulation than the three words, 'Love one another', so long as it is [love] to the end and without exceptions. And then the whole of life is illumined, which is otherwise an abomination and a burden.[6]

Thus she condemned the meanderings of the past, thus she groped her way towards a more authentic future. She was born in December 1891 and was thirty-four years old.[7] She had nineteen years to live.

[5] Sketches in *MMP*. Date of death verified at the cemetery of Ste Geneviève-des-Bois. Hackel, *One, of Great Price* (1965), p. 3 gives the wrong date.

[6] Copy made by S. B. Pilenko, *MMP*.

[7] She was born 8/20 December 1891 in Riga, Livonia (present-day Latvia).

The years to come were to confirm her in the conviction that Nastia's death was a challenge and a turning point. In a subsequent article, which drew on her experience of it, she was to distinguish two different kinds of mourner.

Some are restrained in their sympathy, correct and prosaic: What a misfortune, who would have thought it, I saw him not so long ago, how did it happen, who was his doctor, and so on. In a word, strangers. For others it is not even a question of grief, but the sudden opening of gates into eternity, while the whole of natural existence has lost its stability and its coherence, yesterday's laws have been abolished, desires have faded, meaninglessness has displaced meaning and a different, albeit incomprehensible Meaning has caused wings to sprout at one's back[. . .]. Into the grave's dark maw are plunged all hopes, plans, habits, calculations and, above all, meaning, the whole meaning of life. In the face of this, everything needs to be re-examined or rejected, to be measured against falsehood and corruption.

People call this a visitation of the Lord. A visitation which brings what? Grief? No, more than grief: for he suddenly reveals the true nature of things. And on the one hand we perceive the dead remains of one who was alive[. . .], the mortality of all creation, while on the other hand we simultaneously perceive the life-giving, fiery, all-penetrating and all-consuming Comforter, the Spirit.

But whether such perception can outlast the mourning process is another question:

Eventually, they say, time heals – would it not be more accurate to say 'deadens'? – all. Normality is gradually restored. The soul reverts to its blindness. The gates to eternity are closed once more[. . .].

[Nevertheless] a person may maintain himself on the plane of eternity by acceptance of the new order [revealed]. There is no binding necessity to relapse into everyday life, into the untroubled management of everyday affairs. Let them go their own way, and the light of eternity may yet suffuse them so long as the individual does not grow afraid, does not run away from his own self, does not renounce his awesome fate[. . .], his personal Golgotha, his personal and freely accepted bearing of the cross[. . .].

And I am convinced that anyone who has shared this experience of eternity, if only once; who has understood which way he is going, if only once; who has perceived the One who precedes him, if only once: such a person will find it hard to deviate from this path, to him all comforts will appear ephemeral, all treasures valueless, all companions superfluous if in their midst he fails to see the one Companion, bearing his cross.[8]

There were no half-measures in such an experience. As she once remarked to a friend, 'This sort of visitation fills the soul like an infection, a flood, a fiery furnace.'[9] A poem of the 1930s likewise notes that anguish may have a positive effect:

I thought I was still rich,
the mother of a living child.
But Lord, I must grow poor.
The day of reckoning draws near.

Uproot from my exhausted heart
all earthly hope, elation, fear,
whatever feeds or fills me.
And leave the anguish in command.[10]

By the time she wrote this poem she had passed through the experience a second time. In July 1935, at the age of twenty-one, Gaiana had made the rare and unconventional decision to return to her native land. Initially under the patronage of Aleksei Tolstoi (one of the most favoured writers of Stalin's new establishment who was also one of Liza's friends from days gone by) Gaiana found no difficulty in

[8] *MM* (1947), pp. 134–6.
[9] F. T. Pianov, memoir (1962), *MMP*.
[10] MS, *MMP*; *Stikhi* (1949), pp. 27–8.

readjusting to a new life, nor in finding useful and congenial work.[11] But in June 1936 news reached Paris of her sudden death. In that sombre year of repression it was natural to suspect that she might have been purged. In the event it was made clear that she had died of typhus, and at home.[12] But there was little solace in such supplementary information.

At first Gaiana's mother found the grief unsupportable. 'Once more I do not know/believe,' she noted in a poem of the time, 'I am blinded once again.'[13] 'I shall never forget that painful minute', wrote the priest who told her of the death. 'She rushed out into the street without a word, running. I was afraid she was going to throw herself in the Seine.' Only much later did she return, 'astonishingly pacified'.[14]

She had no access to the grave, in whose dark maw old 'plans, habits and calculations' could have been submerged. In distant Paris a memorial service had to serve in place of a funeral. Liza prostrated herself in prayer throughout. Her fellow-mourners remarked on her composure, despite her obvious desolation. 'It was a great burden', she confided to a friend. 'Black night. The uttermost spiritual isolation[. . .]. Everything was dark all round and only somewhere in the distance was there a minute speck of light. Now I know what death is.'[15]

Part of her experience was communicated in her poetry. It is not surprising that the collection of verse which she published immediately after Gaiana's death should contain a whole section 'On death', the setting for a sequence of poems devoted to Gaiana herself.[16] But she revealed little of their background in her daily life. Not that she was taciturn. On the contrary, she was at ease with most people, eager to engage in conversation, with a humorous (slightly mischie-

---

[11] Letters from Gaiana to her family and friends from the USSR (46), *MMP*.

[12] Letters from Gaiana's (estranged) husband in Moscow to her family (1936), *MMP*.

[13] MS (2 September 1936), *MMP*; *Stikhi* (1937), p. 93.

[14] Archimandrite Lev Gillet, letter to the author (1963).

[15] *Mochul'skii*, p. 70.

[16] *Stikhi* (1937), pp. 84–7, 93.

vous) smile often on her lips. She was tall, handsome, strong and energetic: she gave the impression of a frank, outspoken, generous and easily accessible personality.

Only those who came to know her well were able to perceive that there was an element of reticence in this unexpectedly lonely figure, and that there were thoughts and feelings which she kept in quiet reserve. Of these, the most vital and least frequently discussed were those which concerned Gaiana and her half-sister Nastia, whose full name, Anastasia, means 'resurrection'.

2

A STRAITENING OF THE WAY

The Skobtsovs had met and impetuously married in the abnormal setting of the Russian civil war. At the time each of them was in the public eye. In 1918 she had been responsible for the administration of the town of Anapa on the Black Sea coast. He was a moderate member of the newly established (and short-lived) anti-Bolshevik government of the Kuban: towards the end of its life, in November 1919, he was to be elected president of the Kuban *rada*.[1] In the cold, prosaic daylight of the emigration, the considerable differences between them – social, emotional and intellectual – began to manifest themselves ever more painfully.

Until 1926 concern for Nastia's welfare had provided them with common ground. By contrast, mother and stepfather were divided in their attitude to the adolescent Gaiana. One way or another their differences came to a head in 1927. They agreed to part, and Daniil Skobtsov moved out from the family's damp basement flat in Meudon to find lodgings for himself elsewhere. He took Iura with him.

Meanwhile his wife had acquired new responsibilities which were beginning to bring her out onto that authentic road for which she had hoped at the time of Nastia's death.

It was not to be a literary road. Before the Revolution she had published two volumes of poetry:[2] a third volume was to

---

[1] D. E. Skobtsov was to publish his memoirs of the period towards the end of his life: D. E. Skobtsov, *Tri goda revoliutsii i grazhdanskoi voiny na Kubani* (Paris [1962–5]).

[2] Elizaveta Kuz'mina-Karavaeva, *Skifskie cherepki* (St Petersburg 1912) and *Ruf'* (Petrograd 1916). In addition she published a prose poem, *Iurali* (Petrograd 1915).

be published in 1937.[3] Early in the emigration she also tried her hand at fiction.[4] But from 1927 her publications were to be almost entirely devoted to social and theological questions, mostly with a practical application.[5] And it was in this sphere that she was to find her vocation.

The framework for her new activities was to be provided initially by the Russian Student Christian [in effect Orthodox] Movement in exile which had been founded in 1923.[6] It had its centres in the various capitals of Europe. Its headquarters were in Paris. But the inaccessibility of these metropolitan centres to the Russians scattered in their thousands throughout the industrial backwaters of Europe was soon to cause concern. Several 'peripatetic secretaries' were appointed in order to bring the Movement's missionary, educational and philanthropic work to the provinces, where the need for it was often most acutely felt. One of those appointed (1930) was Liza – more properly, Elizaveta Iur'evna – Skobtsova.

Her travels among Russians in France brought her into contact less with study groups and intellectuals than with impoverished outcasts in an alien setting which had driven many into apathy, resentment or despair. Alcohol was a common refuge for them. The suicide rate was high. 'The Russian Geography of France' on which she wrote for the émigré newspaper *Posledniia Novosti* provided bleak copy. Nevertheless, as she insisted, the dignity even of the most degraded or depraved should not be held in doubt.

'Are they degraded?' [she asked]. Degraded indeed. 'Decayed?' Decaying alive.

---

[3] Monakhinia Mariia, *Stikhi* (Berlin [1937]). There were also to be two posthumous collections, *MM* (1947) and (more important) *Stikhi* (1949). On her poetry of the emigration period see Sergei Hackel, ' "What can we say to God?" The Poetry of Mother Maria Skobtsova (1891–1945)', *Sobornost* 7:5 (1977), pp. 377–84.

[4] Her unfinished novel 'Ravnina russkaia' was published under the name 'Iurii Danilov' in the Parisian journal *Sovremennye zapiski*, No. 19 (1924), pp. 79–133; and No. 20 (1924), pp. 125–215.

[5] See Bibliography (below).

[6] On the foundation of the RSCM see N. Zernov, *The Russian Religious Renaissance of the Twentieth Century* (London 1963), pp. 226–41.

'Drunk, debauched, dishonest, thieving?' Yes and yes again.

'Are they people?' Utterly and undeniably, miserable and abandoned people, whom a human word can [yet] reclaim, so that no trace remains of debauchery or lies.[7]

Liza was to find that she had the capacity to pronounce this word. She was also to find that neither her upbringing as the child of landed gentry, nor her university education, nor her participation in the life of St Petersburg's cultural élite had erected a barrier between herself and those to whom she now addressed herself.

Formally, she might be expected to deliver a lecture to some gathering of exiles in Lyons, Toulouse or Strasbourg. But the demands of the local situation might often overshadow or displace the lecture. 'Experience teaches you to deal with all sorts of unexpected situations', as she explained to a friend:

I would find myself transformed from an official lecturer into a confessor. As soon as I came to know the people we would embark on frank conversations about émigré life or else about the past. And my companions – no doubt sensing me to be a sympathetic listener – would try to find a spare minute afterwards to talk to me alone. A queue would form by the door as if outside a confessional. There would be people wanting to pour out their hearts, to tell of some terrible grief which had burdened them for years, of pangs of conscience which gave them no peace. In such slums it is no use speaking of faith in God, of Christ or of the Church. What is needed here is not religious preaching, but the simplest thing of all: compassion.[8]

Without such compassion, indeed, it would have been impossible sometimes to communicate at all. When she journeyed to the Pyrenean mines to visit refugees who lived and

[7] *Posledniia Novosti* (Paris), 18 June 1932. Other articles in the series appeared on 14 and 24 June.
[8] *Manukhina*, p. 139.

worked there in appalling conditions her proposal to give a talk was understandably met with hostility and silence. One of the miners suggested that she would be more useful if she scrubbed the floor. To his surprise she took him at his word. But as she worked she spilled a bucket of water on herself.

> They just sat and watched. Then suddenly and unexpectedly the man who spoke to me with such bitterness took off his leather jacket and handed it to me: 'You're soaking, put it on'. Then the ice began to break. When I had finished they sat me down at table, brought in the evening meal and we got talking.[9]

At the end of the visit one of the miners confided that he had intended to commit suicide that day. Her arrival had prompted him to postpone, but only to postpone, the plan: 'To live as we live is ridiculous.' Liza took control of him, packed his bags and delivered him to some friends of hers in Toulouse. They welcomed him into their family and with time restored his confidence in life.

It was an unspectacular, yet a fruitful meeting, although – more probably, because – no talk was ever given. She continued to give talks in more appropriate situations as required. But increasingly she came to value and to seek personal encounters such as this.

In the process, risks were usually ignored. 'I remember my first meeting with her some time in the late twenties', wrote P. E. T. Widdrington. 'She had just come back from a visit to Marseilles in which her object was to rescue some Russian intellectuals who had fallen into the opium habit. She had always been fearless and had shown no hesitation raiding a den in the Old City and dragging out two young Russians by force.'[10] But the most prosaic case required as much determination, if not more.

The difficulty was to persevere with each once it had been undertaken. She noted her deficiencies in this respect. 'What

---

[9] Ibid., loc. cit.
[10] P. E. T. Widdrington, memoir, *MMP*. On the Russian colony in Marseilles, see J. H. Simpson, *The Refugee Problem* (London 1939), pp. 307–8.

I give them is negligible', she remarked. 'I talk with them. I leave them. I forget them. But I realize why the results are inadequate. Every one of them demands your whole life, neither more nor less. To give your whole life to some drunkard or cripple, how difficult that is.'[11] Related thoughts are to be found in one of the many poems written while she travelled:

> Again I leave, the poorer,
> for some more distant part.
> The world, try as one might,
> will not fit in one heart.[12]

Whatever the limitations of her help, to give it was to make discoveries. She was gradually establishing a code of practice. It bore little resemblance to the code of those engaged in social service. But it was to inform her work throughout the years to come. It was based on a recognition of the dignity of man created in the 'image and likeness' of God:

> If someone turns with his spiritual world to the spiritual world of another person, he encounters an awesome and inspiring mystery[. . .]. He comes into contact with the true image of God in man, with the very icon of God incarnate in the world, with a reflection of the mystery of God's incarnation and divine manhood. And he needs to accept this awesome revelation of God unconditionally, to venerate the image of God in his brother. Only when he senses, perceives and understands it will yet another mystery be revealed to him – one that will demand his most dedicated efforts[. . .]. He will perceive that this divine image is veiled, distorted and disfigured by the power of evil[. . .]. And he will want to engage in battle with the devil for the sake of the divine image.[13]

But it is a battle which demands self-abnegation. Anyone who engages in it 'should not harbour the slightest desire, however

[11] *Mochul'skii*, p. 68.
[12] MS (1931), *MMP*; *Stikhi* (1949), p. 46.
[13] *Pravoslavnoe Delo* (1939), pp. 40–1.

13

subtle, for personal gain'. By the same token, there should be no question of entertaining any idle curiosity for the victim's experience. On the contrary, it is essential to put oneself in his place, 'to attempt to appreciate and experience from within what he feels, to become all things to all men'.[14]

A doctrinaire approach from without is to be avoided. The reduction of men's needs to a few common denominators is likely to lead to mechanistic and partial solutions. Yet equally pernicious and unprofitable is the facile and sentimental acceptance of the person just as he is, spiritual warts and all. For those who work in this field, 'The balance is achieved by care, sobriety and love'.[15] But this love needs to be extended to the whole person. As was too often forgotten in the Russian Orthodox past, man's body requires care, as well as his spirit and his psyche:

> Man ought to treat the body of his fellow human being with more care than he treats his own. Christian love teaches us to give our fellows material as well as spiritual gifts. We should give them our last shirt and our last piece of bread. Personal almsgiving and the most wide-ranging social work are both equally justified and needed.[16]

Her travels confirmed her in her Christian Socialist convictions. But (although she contributed regularly to A. F. Kerenskii's S-R paper *Dni*)[17] she was little concerned with their political expression. An urgent and, above all, religious sense of mission undergirded her work. A vivid introduction to it is provided by a poem of 1931, in which the day dreams on one of her train journeys through France are suddenly transformed by an acute awareness of the proximity of God.

> Snatches of dreams. Music of the deep.
> Then suddenly a breakthrough to the secret of all secrets.
> Mysteries revealed.

[14] Ibid., pp. 41, 39.
[15] Ibid., p. 39.
[16] Ibid., p. 37.
[17] Issues for 11 November, 9 and 30 December 1928; 3 and 12 May, 9 June 1929, are among those which carry articles by her.

Appearance of the Lord of hosts, the Elohim.

But what can I achieve, almighty Judge?
What am I but a call, a sword in someone else's hand?
A current quickened by the rapids,
a publican who draws attention to men's debts?

Yet you insist on straitening my ways.
'Go, share the life of paupers and of tramps.
And with an everlasting bond
secure yourself to them, the world to me.'[18]

The sense of being an intermediary, a sword in someone else's hand, was not to leave her. In another poem of that same year she asked 'Who am I, Lord?' and provided the answer, 'Only a pretender, broadcasting grace[. . .], distributing sparks from the fire'.[19] As she said to a friend in 1934, 'God has made me into an instrument for others to flourish with my help.'[20]

In the brief anthology of saints' lives which she published in 1927 she went out of her way to stress the importance of such 'instrumentality'. She wrote of Joannicius (ninth century) who was willing to exorcize a possessed girl by accepting possession in her place. She wrote also of Nicephorus (third century), whose life-long friendship with the priest Sapricius had been disrupted by a petty quarrel. Sapricius obstinately refused to be reconciled and the pride which he generated in the course of the quarrel led him to apostatize on the brink of martyrdom. Yet Nicephorus, though rejected and humiliated by his former friend, accepted a martyr's execution in his place and for his sake.[21]

Her narratives were stylized versions of ancient and already stylized tales. But she was taking stock of herself in their light. Nastia's death in the year before their publication had prompted thoughts of a life in which such self-sacrifice might have a mundane application. A few years later Nastia was

[18] *Stikhi* (1949), p. 39.
[19] Ibid., pp. 43–4.
[20] *Mochul'skii*, p. 68.
[21] E. Skobtsova, *Zhatva Dukha* (Paris [1927]), i. 5–14, 23–35.

again to act as a catalyst, this time to bring her to an unconventional and radical decision.

Nastia had been buried near Paris at the Russian cemetery of Ste Geneviève-des-Bois. Subsequently it became possible to purchase a better and more permanent burial plot for her in another section of the same cemetery. But French law required that she be exhumed as well as transferred in the presence of her mother. The latter had thus to re-experience the funeral to the full, and in the aftermath to readjust once more.

It was as she followed her daughter's coffin to its new destination that she came to realize the nature and the scale of the readjustment which the reinterment prompted. The death of her child was unexpectedly enriching and enlarging her maternal role: 'I became aware of a new and special, broad and all-embracing motherhood. I returned from that cemetery a different person. I saw a new road before me and a new meaning in life.' It was a challenging though as yet ill defined prospect: to be 'a mother for all, for all who need maternal care, assistance or protection'.[22] Even so a poem of the early thirties already gives some indication of what her 'extended family' had come to mean.

> You led me up to them and said:
> Adopt these, each with his concern.
> Let them become your life blood,
> bone of your bones, flesh of your flesh.
>
> When I adopted them, I took upon myself
> their aimlessness and pride,
> their endless scuffs and bruises,
> their stubborn childish whims.
>
> Lord, let them no longer blunder
> along those paths where death prevails.
> I speak for them as mother (by your will)
> and their temptations I shoulder as my own.[23]

[22] *Manukhina*, p. 143.
[23] MS, *MMP*; *Stikhi* (1937), p. 23 (with minor variations).

Most of those who shouldered the burdens and temptations of their neighbours in her anthology of lives were early Christian monastics. Consideration of their achievement had also prompted some consideration of their way of life. But could monasticism of a later age conceivably provide the framework for the maternal role to which she was about to dedicate her life? And even if it might, should she or could she – a married woman with two husbands in the background (the one estranged, the other divorced, yet both alive) – proceed to the monastic state? Such complex questions could not be resolved at home, although they were discussed at length. Soon after the reinterment they were to be addressed to her spiritual father, Sergii Bulgakov and to her bishop, Metropolitan Evlogii Georgievskii.

She was fortunate in her advisers. Archpriest Sergii Bulgakov (1871–1944) had first come into prominence at the turn of the century as an economist. He was then a 'legal' Marxist. That he would complete his career as an Orthodox theologian could not have been foreseen. He was to be distinguished in both spheres of life, conformist in neither. Yet the independence of his work was invariably the fruit of integrity and erudition. These qualities helped to determine his progress *From Marxism to Idealism* (the title of a volume which he published in 1903), to argue persuasively for the reconciliation of the Russian intelligentsia with the Church (1909) and, eventually, to effect his own. His ordination to the priesthood took place in Moscow during the tense summer of 1918. He was not to remain there for long. Even as a Marxist he had incurred Lenin's ire in 1899 for his 'revisionist' treatment of Marx on agriculture. As a Christian apologist there was still less to commend him to the new establishment. On 1 January 1923 he was expelled from the Soviet state. Thus it proved possible for him in 1925 to join the staff of the newly founded Orthodox Theological Institute of St Sergius in Paris.[24] As its professor of dogmatics and dean he was to remain there for the rest of his life, and it was there that Liza Skobtsova came

[24] For an outline of the Institute's history see D. A. Lowrie, *Saint Sergius in Paris: The Orthodox Theological Institute* (London 1954).

to know him. But much as she learned to appreciate Bulgakov the theologian (she attended his lectures at the Institute and was familiar with his prolific published work), it was Bulgakov the priest for whom she had a particular affection and regard. In him she discovered a mentor who, notwithstanding his powerful personality, 'never imposed his authority on his disciples, for his love of freedom and his respect for the individual made him a firm supporter and a trusted adviser, [. . .] never a master demanding unquestioning obedience'.[25]

The Theological Institute had been established under the auspices of Metropolitan Evlogii (1868–1946), the ruling bishop of a considerable section of the Russian diaspora in Western Europe and the exarch successively of two patriarchates: Moscow (1921–31/1945–6) and Constantinople (1931–45).[26] In the Russian Church his task was without precedent. Fortunately the diaspora gained in him an experienced administrator: he had already spent thirteen years in the episcopate before his emigration in 1920. Those years had also seen a considerable broadening of his sympathies. In the diaspora he proved to be a pastor with remarkable insight, tolerance and tact. As one of his clergy put it, 'Everybody had access to him and placed on his shoulders any spiritual or material burden. He entered with sympathy into every individual problem[. . .]. He wanted to give everybody the possibility of following his or her own call.'[27]

Both of Liza's advisers were prepared to countenance an unconventional answer to her questions. But neither had the inclination to impose one. The necessary scrutiny of possible

[25] N. Zernov, *The Russian Religious Renaissance of the Twentieth Century* (London 1963), p. 142. For a survey of Bulgakov's work as theologian see L. A. Zander, *Bog i mir* (Paris 1948). No biography exists as yet.

[26] The situation of the persecuted Church in the USSR made it increasingly more difficult for Metropolitan Evlogii to act as its official representative; hence his resignation as exarch in 1931 and his canonical submission to the Patriarch of Constantinople (*Evlogii*, pp. 618–29). The improvement of Church-State relations during the Second World War persuaded him to revert to the Moscow patriarchate in the last year of his life.

[27] Igumen Lev Gillet in *Sobornost*, NS 34 (1946), p. 5.

18

objections to her plan made her feel that 'the barriers were insurmountable'.[28]

At least it was not difficult to establish that the barriers were not set up by Canon Law. The Orthodox *Nomocanon* in xiv titles (ii. 4) of the seventh-ninth centuries (which in its turn validated the 22nd and 117th *Novellae* of the Emperor Justinian) made provision for divorce should either party in a marriage seek to embark on the monastic life.[29] But it was one thing to make the decision, another to gain the partner's assent. Daniil Skobtsov was not enthusiastic. It needed the Metropolitan to persuade him. It was fortunate that the matter could be resolved the more speedily and economically since there was no need to involve the French courts. They for their part would only have been bemused by the Byzantine law which Evlogii now brought into play.

An ecclesiastical divorce was promulgated on the anniversary of Nastia's death, 7 March 1932. Preparations for the monastic profession were begun. A second-hand cassock was obtained. A date was fixed. And inwardly (as she wrote), 'Everything is checked, my inventory prepared[. . .]. Everything is checked and nothing keeps me here.'[30]

On the appointed day later that same month, in the gallery of the chapel at the Theological Institute off the rue de Crimée (XIXe), Elizaveta Iur'evna Skobtsova, née Pilenko, by her first marriage Kuz'mina-Karavaeva, put aside her secular clothes, vested herself in a simple white garment and descended the dark stairs into the chapel to prostrate herself in the form of a cross on the floor.

> Dressed as I am in white
> my inner self still bears
> the name Elizaveta. Then
> tomorrow I'll be simply *N*.[31]

[28] *Mochul'skii*, p. 72.
[29] *Corpus iuris civilis*, ed. P. Krueger *et al.* (Berlin 1954), iii. 150 and 562 (*Novellae* xxii. 5 and cxvii. 12, dated respectively 536 and 542).
[30] *Stikhi* (1949), p. 32.
[31] Ibid., p. 33.

3

MONASTICISM

Metropolitan Evlogii himself officiated at the service of monastic profession and it was he who gave the traditional exhortation.

> Love nothing more than God. Thou shalt not love father or mother or brethren or any of thy kin, thou shalt not love thyself more than God: nor the kingdom of the world, nor any kind of ease or honour. Evade not poverty: rather abide in it to thy life's end[. . .]. Fix thy mind constantly on the good things which are reserved for those who live in God. Be mindful of the martyrs and monastic saints who have ever striven to obtain them by their many labours and their pains, by their frequent sacrifice of blood and life[. . .]. Be watchful in all respects. Endure all things as a good soldier of Christ. For our Lord himself, being rich in mercy, became poor for our sakes that we might be enriched with his kingdom. Therefore ought we to imitate him, to suffer all things for his sake, to continue in his commandments day and night. For the Lord himself said, If any man will come after me, let him deny himself and take up his cross and follow me: that is, let him be ready ever to obey his commandments, even unto death.

The challenging words of the exhortation provided her with guidelines. Only in retrospect was it possible to discern how aptly the ancient words corresponded to her future:

> Wherefore it is necessary for thee to bear hunger and thirst, reproach and grief, disgrace and persecution, and to be burdened by many another sorrow whereby is manifest the life in God. And when all this suffering comes upon

thee, rejoice, saith the Lord, for great is thy reward in heaven.

The postulant's new name was now brought into use. Elizaveta was to be replaced by Maria. Maria was ceremonially vested. The Metropolitan then placed a cross in her right hand.

Receive, sister Maria, the shield of faith, the cross of Christ[. . .]; constantly remember that the Lord said, Whoever will come after me, let him deny himself and take up his cross and follow me.

Into her left hand he placed a lighted candle:

For the Lord said, Let your light so shine before men that they may see your good works and glorify your Father which is in heaven.[1]

As the service began, so it ended, with a chant on the subject of the Prodigal Son. But whereas the earlier chant spoke of the Son's penitential approach and appeal to the Father, the conclusion dwelt only on the joy occasioned by the Prodigal's return and restoration.[2]

For the new Mother Maria, as for the Prodigal, it was a joy to be shared. Her earlier intention to keep her monastic profession a secret had been abandoned during the three days' vigil which preceded the event. But her friends were urged to forget her past. 'Make no attempt to harbour the image of my former self', she wrote. The writings of this former self – 'all forgotten notebooks, articles and poems' – should be burnt.[3]

Fortunately she herself did not proceed wholeheartedly with any such destructive measures.[4] Nor did she abandon poetry as such. But although she continued to write she main-

[1] *Posledovanie inocheskago postrizheniia* (Rome 1952), pt. ii, pp. 22–4, 38–9.
[2] Ibid., pt. ii, pp. 14, 46.
[3] MS of a poem (1932), *MMP*; first published in Hackel, *MM* (1980), p. 48.
[4] Certainly, poems of the years 1930–2 have survived. The almost complete disappearance of MSS from the 1920s needs a separate explanation.

21

tained a diplomatic silence on the subject. It was a silence to be broken only at Gaiana's death.[5]

Whatever the significance of the instructions that her work be burnt – they were themselves enshrined in a poem – they conveyed the false impression that rearguard actions were required to disengage her from the past. In actual fact, the positive nature and effect of her profession were to remain evident throughout the months and years to come.

In January 1933 Metropolitan Evlogii met the literary scholar Konstantin Mochul'skii at a weekend conference organized by Mother Maria. 'As you can see,' he remarked, 'Mother Maria was tonsured, and she has been radiant ever since.'[6]

Eighteen months after the event she herself could say, 'Altogether everything has become simpler, very simple, very. And there is less rhetoric. In fact, no room left for rhetoric at all.'[7] By rhetoric she meant not only speech, but any activity which was superfluous, disproportionate or suspect.

However, the profession which had brought her a new simplicity and equilibrium had not determined the means by which she should 'share the life of paupers and of tramps'. For the time being, the room which was put at her disposal by Lev and Valentina Zander in their flat at Clamart provided her with a temporary haven where she could ponder the possibilities and prepare for her work.

Metropolitan Evlogii had placed high hopes on Mother Maria. 'I was glad,' he wrote in respect of her monastic profession, 'and hoped that she would become the founder of convent life in the emigration.'[8] For her part Mother Maria

[5] Soon after Gaiana's death she published three poems in the prestigious *Sovremennye zapiski*, No. 62 (1936), pp. 185–7. The following year was to see the publication of her collection *Stikhi* (1937).
[6] *Mochul'skii*, p. 65. K. V. Mochul'skii (1892–1948) was to become one of Mother Maria's closest friends and collaborators. His succinct memoir on her (published 1946) remains the most perceptive short account of her life. On their friendship see M. Kantor's preface to K. V. Mochul'skii, *Aleksandr Blok* (Paris 1948), pp. 9–10.
[7] *Mochul'skii*, p. 67.
[8] *Evlogii*, p. 566.

valued the Metropolitan's confidence and support. 'My great-est joy is the thoroughly exceptional understanding of all my schemes on the Metropolitan's part', she wrote in a letter of June 1932. 'With his help you could really move mountains, given the will and the strength.'[9] It was not yet clear to either party that none of these schemes was to lead to the establish-ment or development of traditional convent life.

In the summer of 1932 Mother Maria set out for Latvia and Estonia on behalf of the Russian SCM. In these former provinces of the Russian Empire, now independent republics, Orthodox monasteries and convents survived unaffected by the persecution of religion across the border in the USSR. Mother Maria was able to experience traditional monastic life at first hand and to measure herself against it.

At the communities which she visited – they included the Dormition convent at Piukhtitsa and the Trinity convent in her native Riga[10] – she was received with interest and affec-tion. In Riga, though her stay was a brief one, she was even fitted and presented with a cassock of her own. But their way of life did not impress her. As she wrote on her return to France,

> There is undoubtedly much personal piety in them, indi-vidual striving after God, possibly even individual sanctity; but as authentic organisms, as entities [. . .] they simply do not exist. The significance of these frontier monasteries and convents is beyond dispute: they safeguard precepts, they conserve vast hoards bequeathed them from the past, [they conserve] the precious treasure chest of ritual splendour and tradition. They may be expected to preserve them to the end. But that is all that can be expected.[11]

In private conversation she dismissed them as 'bourgeois': 'No one [there] is aware that the world is on fire. There is no

[9] Letter to her mother and children, *MMP*.
[10] Both convents (now within the borders of the USSR) remain open (1981).
[11] *Novyi Grad*, No. 5 (1932), p. 96. Mother Maria was to revisit Riga at the beginning of 1935. But there is no indication that she called at the Trinity convent on this occasion.

concern for the fate of the world.'[12] By contrast, her own monastic profession had, if anything, increased her apprehension of imminent disaster:

> They changed my name
> and took away my patronymic
> thus making me God's child.
> And these are prophecies I hear
> when I am all alone and calm and quiet:
> They are near the days of sorrow,
> they are near.[13]

She returned to France with the conviction that a new type of monasticism was required, better suited to the needs and circumstances of the emigration. It was to be neither introspective, nor secure.

> Everyone is always faced [. . .] with the necessity of choosing between the comfort and warmth of an earthly home, well protected from winds and storms, and the limitless expanse of eternity, which contains only one sure and certain item. And this one sure and certain item is a cross.[14]

By contrast, the traditional monastic community too often generated, cherished and preferred precisely such 'comfort and warmth':

> In the majority of cases, the vow of chastity [. . .] brings into monastic life people who have no family life of their own, people who have built up no private life, and who have not perceived to what extent the absolute independence of a private life is utterly incompatible with the eschatologically oriented spirit of monasticism. An extremely curious development has taken place, and the foundations of monastic life have been gradually transformed.
>
> The desire to create a family is more than an urge to satisfy physical instincts, more than an earthly yearning for

[12] Quoted by F. T. Pianov, memoir (1968), MS, *MMP*.
[13] *Stikhi* (1949), p. 34.
[14] *MM* (1947), p. 136.

love or even for parenthood. A family is also based on another instinct, one which is extremely potent in the human psyche: the urge to build a nest, to organize and shape a private life which can be shut off from the outside world behind walls and locked in by strong bolts. As someone evolves a way of life, he concerns himself not only with his material welfare, but also with the moral purity of his life, with its inner beauty. He protects it against any filth or pollution from without [. . .], while within its bounds he asserts his individual 'I' and his family's collective 'we' in opposition to any external 'they'.

Those who in all sincerity take the vow of chastity reject one element that would normally impel them towards the establishment of a family: they accept everything else that is basic to the establishment of family life. They want an organized and separate life, a household in common, high walls through which the filth and misery of the world will not penetrate. They establish a kind of spiritual family and shield it from any interference as something sacred.

Mother Maria allows that a life devoted to the sustenance of such a family might have been acceptable in past ages, though even then there were hermits and Fools for Christ's sake who rejected order so as to serve God and man in greater freedom. But the present (as she was to write in 1938) is least of all conducive to the 'family' model of monastic life.

When time itself becomes the harbinger of apocalyptic events, when mankind is truly led to Golgotha, when there are no paths, no stability in the world: in such an epoch as ours, is it possible to accept the normal, traditional, spiritual monasticism of the past as a necessary yardstick for monasticism's future? No, it is not. And hard as it is to protest against the magnificent and beautiful principle of a loving monastic family, separated from the world, [. . .] yet the protest must be made. An inner voice insists that covetousness be rejected in this sphere as in any other.

25

But the alternative is not another system. On the contrary, renewal demands anarchy and folly:

> Open your gates to homeless thieves, let the outside world sweep in to demolish your magnificent liturgical system, abase yourself, empty yourself, make yourself of no account. However much [you do so], can your self-abasement and degradation ever compare to Christ's? Accept the vow of poverty in all its devastating severity: destroy all comfort, even monastic comfort[. . .].
>
> There are times when all that has been said cannot be made obvious and clear since the atmosphere around us is a pagan one and we are tempted by its idolatrous charms. But our times are firmly in tune with Christianity in that suffering is part of their nature. They demolish and destroy in our hearts all that is stable, mature, hallowed by the ages and treasured by us. They help us genuinely and utterly to accept the vow of poverty, to seek no rule, but rather anarchy, the anarchic life of Fools for Christ's sake, seeking no monastic enclosure, but the complete absence of even the subtlest barrier which might separate the heart from the world and its wounds.[15]

Indeed, it was the world and its wounds which had originally brought her to monasticism. The latter could not exclude or supersede the former. If she had ever been placed in a position which required her to choose *between* monasticism and a life of service, the life of service would have been preferred. Metropolitan Evlogii was subsequently to acknowledge that 'she made her profession in order to give herself unreservedly to social work'. Had he perceived this at the outset he would have spared himself some disappointment. 'She called her social work "monasticism in the world" ', wrote Evlogii (himself a monk who had rarely lived for any time within the framework of a community). 'But monasticism in the strict sense of the term, with its ascesis and its inner prayer, was something which she not only failed to

[15] *Novyi Grad*, No. 13 (1938), pp. 149–52; reprinted in *MM* (1947), pp. 119–23.

26

understand, but went so far as to reject, considering it out-dated and unnecessary. I never managed to explain to her the inner meaning of monasticism[. . .].'[16]

Not suprisingly, 'those who cherished the ideal of strictly regulated monasticism as codified in ascetical literature and in the demanding statutes of community life were not able to find a way in common with her', commented Tatiana Manukhina. 'The older she grew and spiritually the more mature, the less she acted the part of a nun.'[17] Or rather, to borrow her own more positive terminology, 'At present monastics possess only one monastery, the whole wide world.'[18] At the same time, 'The more we go out into the world, the more we give ourselves to the world, the less we are of the world. For the worldly do not give the world an offering of themselves.'[19]

---

[16] *Evlogii*, pp. 541, 566.
[17] *Manukhina*, p. 152.
[18] 'On monasticism' (1937), *MMP*. It is possible that the phrase was borrowed from Evlogii. According to S. B. Pilenko (MS note, *MMP*), the Metropolitan once remarked 'For your work the whole world is a monastery'.
[19] 'On monasticism' (1937), *MMP*.

4

THE HOUSE AT RUE DE LOURMEL

Mother Maria was known to enjoy a traditional tale about St Nicholas and St John Cassian. The two of them had returned to earth one day to see how things were going. They came across a peasant whose cart had slipped into a muddy ditch. The peasant asked for help. Cassian regretfully refused: he would soon be on his way back to the heavenly realm and his robes had to be spotlessly white. Nicholas said nothing. He was already up to his knees in the mud, exerting all his strength to help the peasant in his need. When God learned the reason for the spotless vestments of the one and the filthy condition of the other, he ordered the church calendar to be rearranged. Hence to this day St Nicholas is annually commemorated twice (9 May and 6 December). But Cassian's feast (relegated to 29 February) recurs only once in four years.[1]

The story suits her. She disdained any kind of sartorial refinement and dressed as simply as she could. She would have preferred to wear a nondescript length of canvas with an opening for the head and a rope as a belt.[2] As it was, her cassock (whether second-hand or – on that rare occasion – new) usually bore the traces of whatever work she had been engaged on in the recent past. Moreover the work itself brought help to numerous peasants who were caught in the mire, the slough of despond: it was the kind of help which, as she wrote, necessarily involves 'the renunciation of white garb'.[3] As Tagore would have put it, 'What harm is there if thy clothes become tattered and stained?'

[1] The relevant dates are given in *Pravoslavnyi tserkovnyi kalendar' 1980* (Moscow 1980), pp. 18, 33 and 70.
[2] *Manukhina*, p. 154.
[3] E. Iu. Skobtsova in *Dni*, 7 September 1930.

Leave this chanting and singing and telling of beads! Whom dost thou worship in this lonely dark corner of a temple with doors all shut? Open thine eyes and see thy God is not before thee!

He is there where the tiller is tilling the hard ground and where the path-maker is breaking stones. He is with them in sun and in shower, and his garment is covered with dust. Put off thy holy mantle and even like him come down on the dusty soil!

Deliverance? Where is this deliverance to be found? Our master himself has joyfully taken upon him the bonds of creation; he is bound with us all for ever.

Come out of thy meditations and leave aside thy flowers and incense! What harm is there if thy clothes become tattered and stained? Meet him and stand by him in toil and in sweat of thy brow.[4]

Certainly there was no turning aside from God involved in turning thus towards his tillers and path-makers. 'The way to God lies through love of people, and there is no other way', she said to Mochul'skii.

At the Last Judgement I shall not be asked whether I was successful in my ascetic exercises, how many bows and prostrations I made [in the course of prayer]. I shall be asked, Did I feed the hungry, clothe the naked, visit the sick and the prisoners. That is all I shall be asked. About every poor, hungry and imprisoned person the Saviour says 'I': 'I was hungry and thirsty, I was sick and in prison'. To think that he puts an equal sign between himself and

[4] Rabindranath Tagore, *Gitanjali (Song Offerings)* (London 1913), pp. 8–9. Tagore would have been familiar to Mother Maria from the Russian translations of his work, which enjoyed considerable popularity on the eve of the Revolution. Two different Moscow publishers issued his collected works (1912–17 and 1915). *Gitanjali* had appeared in a fourth edition by 1918.

anyone in need. . . . I always knew it, but now it has somehow penetrated to my sinews. It fills me with awe.[5]

It was an experience which came to dominate her thoughts and actions, leaving little room for any chanting or telling of beads. Instead, to work – much to the relief of her friends Nikolai Berdiaev (1874–1948) and Fedor Pianov (1889–1969), who had earlier feared that traditional monasticism might shackle or disillusion her. 'I must confess that I did not sympathize greatly with her decision to accept monasticism', wrote Berdiaev. 'I did not consider it to be her vocation and [feared that] she would be confronted with so many difficulties by the church hierarchy that, with her uncompromising character, she might perhaps be forced to abandon monasticism – a very painful prospect.' With such reservations, both Berdiaev and Pianov had attempted to dissuade her from her decision to become a nun. By way of a protest Pianov was even to absent himself from her profession. The latter (in Berdiaev's words) was to be followed by 'a honeymoon phase in her monastic life'. But (as he noted with some satisfaction) 'it was not long before her freedom-loving and rebellious nature came to the fore.'[6]

There was no lack of work to be done. Provisions made for refugees by the French governments of the 1930s were not ungenerous. Indeed a well-researched Chatham House report of 1939 went out of its way to note that 'no European country approaches France in the numbers to whom permanent refuge has been given. She treats her refugees with liberality and consideration.'[7] However, not all were equally entitled to benefit from this liberality. Nor was the state invariably well placed to exercise it in a decade of mounting unemployment. It was unfortunate that the one thing which so many of the most disadvantaged refugees lacked – a fixed domicile – was regarded as a basic requirement for anyone seeking to apply

[5] *Mochul'skii*, pp. 70–1 (referring to Matt. 25:35, 42–3); cf. *Pravoslavnoe Delo* (1939), p. 30.
[6] N. A. Berdiaev in *Russkie Novosti* (1 April 1966), p. 2.
[7] J. H. Simpson, *The Refugee Problem* (London 1939), p. 298.

for state assistance with clothing, food or fuel: 'The position of a refugee without a fixed domicile is quite a different one and he must apply to private organizations for assistance.'[8] A number of such organizations existed already.[9] Mother Maria was eventually to establish another. But her first concern was to provide a fixed domicile, if only for a limited number of people.

Her first house at 9 villa de Saxe, Paris VIIe (an inappropriately prosperous district, with the Hôtel des Invalides at its centre) was leased – like all her foundations – without secure financial backing. 'No matter', she remarked to a friend: '[. . .] we need to walk on the waters. The apostle Peter did so, after all, and he didn't drown. Of course it is safer to go round by land, but you may never reach your destination.'[10] She recorded comparable thoughts in her notebook:

There are two ways to live. Completely legitimately and respectably it is possible to walk on dry land: to measure, to weigh and to plan ahead. But it is also possible to walk on the waters. Then it becomes impossible to measure or to plan ahead, the one thing necessary is to believe all the time. An instant of doubt, and you begin to sink.[11]

Yet on the morning of the day appointed for the signing of the lease her optimism had not brought in even the sum required for her deposit. Her one hope lay in a last-minute appeal to the Metropolitan. By the end of the day she was able to write to her mother:

Today I signed a contract for the lease of a vast and

[8] *Report of the Nansen International Office for Refugees for the year ending June 30th 1935* (Geneva 1935), Appendix i, p. 15.
[9] Among such organizations may be mentioned *Centre d'Aide Sociale* (directed by S. M. Zernova); the Committee for Social Assistance to Emigrés organized by the Russian SCM; the Russian Red Cross; *Union des Mutilés et Invalides Russes*; *Union française d'Aide aux Russes* (directed by Mlle Carlier); and *Zemgor* [*Rossiiskii Zemsko-Gorodskoi komitet pomoshchi bezhentsam*].
[10] *Manukhina*, pp. 144–5.
[11] Entry for 31 August 1934, MS notebook, *MMP*.

remarkable house. Until the last moment I did not believe it would be possible, I was incredibly nervous; there was a host of major problems, the worst of which involved the finances being placed in jeopardy at the very last minute. Now all this is in the past (today the Metropolitan gave me five thousand [francs], which I duly paid over to the owner), I can already spend the night at home[. . .]. Soon I shall have a great deal of work – but work of a joyful sort, for all this is no longer a fantasy, but solid reality, miraculous as it seems[. . .]. What a remarkable person Metropolitan Evlogii is. He understands everything absolutely, like no one else on this earth.[12]

'I can already spend the night at home': she moved immediately into a house full of promise, but devoid even of the simplest furniture. Only a lone piano stood in the hall, incongruous not only because of its dream-like isolation, but also because of the new lessee's complete indifference to music.[13] At the outset she slept on blankets on the floor. A large icon of a favourite feast (the *Pokrov*) stood against the wall beside her. A pile of telephone directories acted as a chair. At first there was no electricity or gas.

The regular chiming of bells in the convent of Poor Clares next door,[14] the quiet and regulated movement of the sisters past its windows on the way to prayer, provided an intriguing contrast to her own incipient 'anarchy for Christ's sake'. At the same time her first (and as yet solitary) meals were invested with a rare dignity: so much so that their eucharistic associations could provoke intimations of the mysterious Bridegroom whose arrival is delayed until the middle of the night (Matt. 25:1–13).

[12] Undated letter (1932), *MMP*.
[13] This was something that her mother, who had been a gifted singer, found cause to regret at the end of her days. 'There was no point in teaching her the piano', she remarked in a reference to her daughter's schooldays (S. B. Pilenko [*o.* 1960]).
[14] The convent remains in its original place (5–7 villa de Saxe); the house occupied by Mother Maria has been demolished.

At last. Quickly lock the door.
Neglected household.
Daylight hardly penetrates the dusty panes.
Somewhere mice are busy in the straw.

I shall sweep the rubbish from the corners,
scrub the table clean,
gather up the remnants of forgotten thoughts,
feed the remnants to the flames.

This is to be a house,
and not some airless den. A home.
I shall take a plate and cut some bread.
In a cup I shall dilute some wine.

I shall sit, my brow propped on my hands.
No longer is the twilight visible outside.
I have the foolish virgins on my mind,
the story of the oil found lacking in their lamps.

The day was murky and the sunset slow.
Then night. The silence mumbling.
At the approach of dawn the air is tense with cold.
My body has no wish to battle against sleep.

If only sleep would not constrict my will.
There is the smell of chilly silence from the floor.
I can hardly see the window frames.
The dark is sonorous, pervasive, deep.

Spirit, intensify the struggle at this time.
Quiet: a knock. Soon time for day to break.
My icon lamp is lit, the wick well primed with oil.
My guest is at the door. A vast wind in his wake.[15]

The 'neglected household' was soon to be transformed.
Within weeks it was furnished on gifts and cast-offs, as well
as bargains for which she hunted with enthusiasm. Hardly
was it furnished before it became a flourishing centre. To
make more room for residents (mostly young Russian women
who were out of work) Mother Maria left her own room and
slept by the boiler. She invited Mochul'skii to visit her 'cell'

[15] *Stikhi* (1937), pp. 49–50.

and 'to sit among the ashes': 'She is tucked into a little corner behind the boiler for the central heating. A narrow iron bedstead; a hole in the floor, stuffed with an old boot: a rat lives there.'[16] As Tatiana Manukhina noted, 'She already had nothing of her own, nor did she want anything; the very fact that she possessed nothing, not even a room of her own, made her happy.'[17]

One of the rooms on the first floor was set aside as a domestic chapel, for which Mother Maria herself painted an icon screen. The spacious dining room on the ground floor served as a common room. This would house discussion groups and lectures. The former might be unpretentious and uninspiring; the latter would involve speakers of exceptional importance such as Bulgakov and Berdiaev. There would also be occasional weekend conferences. But the residents were under no obligation to participate either in services or discussions. Their principal need was for a stable and a caring environment. This above all was what their warden strove to provide. 'I get tired,' she wrote to her mother, 'but I am content with my venture.'[18]

Within two years the venture had outgrown the premises. Furthermore, its founder had new schemes in mind. In September 1934 a move was made to a larger, but more derelict house, which had stood abandoned for many a year. It was more humbly situated in the fifteenth *arrondissement*, where many Russians had settled: not only was it an inexpensive area, its unemployed received the dole. Mother Maria's new address (which was to become a by-word in émigré Paris) was 77 rue de Lourmel.

It was one thing to move, another to secure the rent. A metropolitan's subvention could hardly be expected once again. In any case it could never cover twenty thousand francs a year. 'She has no money, the risk is enormous,' noted Mochul'skii, 'but she is not afraid.' She herself preferred to speak in different terms:

[16] *Mochul'skii*, p. 65.
[17] *Manukhina*, p. 147.
[18] Undated letter (1932), *MMP*.

You think I am fearless. It is not that. I simply know that this is needed and that it will exist. At Saxe I have no room to spread myself. At present I feed twenty-five hungry people, there I shall be able to feed a hundred. There are simply times when I can feel the Lord taking me by the scruff of my neck and compelling me to do what he wants. That's how it is now with this house. From a sober point of view this would be considered madness[. . .]. To an outsider I might seem reckless. I don't mind. Rather than make calculations, I submit.[19]

At Lourmel there were some brick stables in the yard. A photograph of the time shows them housing a lorry of some size.[20] Mother Maria removed the remnants of the stalls (together with a goodly quantity of refuse) and converted the structure into a church. Her efforts transformed the unpromising interior. Gradually the walls were brought to life by embroidery, an art in which she excelled. A large Life of David was soon to decorate the south wall;[21] a remarkable Last Supper was eventually to crown the Royal Doors, embroidered (as always without any preliminary design) during the difficult years 1940–1.[22] The vestments were also embroidered (as well as sewn) by her.

Many of the icons were her own work. Others were painted by Sister Ioanna Reitlinger. Some were the fruit of their collaboration. The church was to serve a substantial, albeit ever-diminishing community for more than thirty years.[23]

Lamp post No. 559 of the fifteenth *arrondissement* threw light onto the shabby exterior of the house itself. The stucco crum-

---

[19] *Mochul'skii*, p. 69.

[20] One of several photographs showing Lourmel on the eve, and in the process, of restoration, *MMP*.

[21] Present location: the monastery of St John the Baptist at Tolleshunt Knights (Essex). Detail reproduced in Hackel, *One, of Great Price* (1965), p. 84.

[22] At present in the author's care. Detail reproduced on plate 16.

[23] Towards the end of the 1960s a section of the street was 'developed'. Both the church and the house at 77 rue de Lourmel were demolished. Nos. 77–85 now form a single block of offices and flats. The Lourmel congregation was disbanded in 1973.

bled from walls which, with their plaster rosettes and classical pilasters, had obviously seen better times. It was now as undistinguished as most of its neighbours in a largely lower-middle and working class district. Yet it differed from them in no longer shutting out the world at large. On the contrary, the welcome it provided could mean all the difference between survival and collapse for those 'least favoured in the fight for existence'.

> The house is roomy, but dusty, grubby, humble, unattractive; yet it is all redeemed by its warm sense of shelter, security and gratifying huddling together in this salvatory Noah's ark, which has nothing to fear from the waves of life's threatening elements, from the horror of rent overdue, of the penury and despair of unemployment. Here one can wait awhile, regain one's breath and gain temporary shelter until the time comes to stand on one's own two feet again.[24]

Lourmel was to become and to remain the centre of Mother Maria's activities. But other houses were to be added to it at various times. Not all were to serve the same purpose, not all were to be equally successful. At 43 rue François Gérard (XVIe) a large house was set aside for families who needed accommodation. More humble premises at 74 rue de Félix Faure (XVe) were provided for single men (and the now 'single' Daniil Skobtsov was to lodge there for a time). Most important, a spacious country house at Noisy-le-Grand (Seine-et-Oise) was to be transformed into a sanatorium for consumptives: as an old-age home it was to survive them all.[25]

At Lourmel there was a hostel for the needy and, independent of it, a canteen. By 1937 something like three dozen residents were lodged in the house, 'part of whom pay their way, while others find it impossible to contribute even half their dues [. . .]. [Others] justify their keep by one form of work or another.'

[24] *Manukhina*, p. 150.
[25] It survives into the 1980s under the auspices of the municipality of Noisy-le-Grand, but without any detriment to its character as a Russian Orthodox foundation. See chapter 5, below.

Attached to the women's home at 77 rue [de] Lourmel a cheap canteen has existed for some three years at which from a hundred to a hundred and twenty dinners are served per day. The cost of the dinner (soup and main course with meat) was raised this autumn [1936] from one and a half to two francs. The canteen is frequented mostly by those who receive the dole.[26]

At the same time, the employed who did not qualify for the dole received their dinner free of charge.[27] As a reporter from *Posledniia Novosti* noted, there were 22,991 dinners served in the course of 1935: their popularity was marked by an increase from 814 dinners in January to 2,815 in December that same year. But it was not only the price or quality of the food (nor the unlimited quantity of free bread supplied by a sympathetic Polish baker) which attracted customers. Everything was done to avoid any suggestion of soup-kitchen charity or condescension.[28] Thus the customer's self-esteem was enhanced and not only his body nourished.

However much Mother Maria disliked routine, the daily foraging for food, together with its preparation and distribution, came to occupy a considerable proportion of her time.

Part of her routine had already been established at villa de Saxe. Well before dawn she would set out for Les Halles, then the central markets of Paris (the 'belly of Paris', in Zola's phrase). She brought a sack with her, and this was to be filled as daylight broke with all the odds and ends – particularly perishable goods – which were then sold off cheaply or simply donated to charities or to the poor. She was well known at Les Halles. Fish, bones, over-ripe fruit and vegetables past their prime were poured into her capacious container. This was eventually to be heaved onto her shoulders and taken via one of the early Metro trains to her kitchen. A wheelbarrow would be welcome, she remarked once: on the previous day

[26] *Vestnik. Organ tserkovno-obshchestvennoi zhizni* (1937), No. 1–2, pp. 24–5.
[27] Mother Elizaveta [S.V.] Medvedeva, memoir (1970), *MMP*.
[28] See a reporter's comments in the paper *Illiustrirovannaia Rossiia*, 13 July 1935.

fish had soaked the sack and she still carried the smell of it with her. A barrow would prevent that sort of thing.[29]

In this shabby nun 'with the sleeve of her dusty cassock torn and well-worn men's shoes on her feet'[30] it was difficult to recognize the poet, the intellectual, the once prosperous lady who in her youth had never been required to concern herself with where or how the servants bought the household's food.

The kitchen was not usually to occupy her to the same degree. Gaiana was available to supervise it in its early days. But it was not always easy to find a regular replacement for her after she left for the USSR. Manukhina found Mother Maria one tropical day in July at the red-hot stove, stirring a vast cauldron of cabbage soup. She was barefooted and (contrary to custom) bareheaded: for the best part of six months she had hardly left the kitchen.

At times when the kitchen made lesser demands on her, her room under the back stairs served as a consulting room for visitors. To reach it they would leave the black and white tiled floor of the entrance hall and follow brown and beige tiles into a dark passage which led to the kitchen. On the right, just before the kitchen, was her door.

The room in which Mother Maria lives is under the stairs, between the kitchen and the hall [wrote Mochul'skii]. In it stands a large table, littered with books, manuscripts, letters, bills, and a quantity of utterly incongruous objects. There is a basket of different coloured balls of wool, a bowl with some cold unfinished tea. A large portrait of Gaiana on the wall over the divan. Bookshelves, cupboards, an old armchair with its stuffing hanging out. The room is unheated. The door is always open. There are times when Mother [Maria] can no longer bear it, she locks the door, drops into the armchair and says, 'I can't go on like this, I can't take anything in, I'm tired, I really am tired. There

[29] *Manukhina*, p. 146.
[30] *Mochul'skii*, p. 75. A photograph of the shoes is given in T. Stratton Smith, *The Rebel Nun* (London 1965), p. 126.

have been about forty people here today, each with his own
sorrow and needs. After all, I can't chase them away.' But
locking the door is no solution. Persistent knocking begins.
Mother opens the door and says to me, 'There you are,
that's how I live'.[31]

According to Bulgakov, the place was a Hermitage for dis-
oriented Stumblers, *Shatalovo pustyn'*. Its clients would arrive
throughout the day and well into the night.

The sudden death of an émigré chauffeur left his widow
homeless. She came to Lourmel. There was no spare bed.
Mother Maria gave up her own and spent night after night
talking her through her distress. Such nights did not exhaust
her. Far from it: 'I feel extraordinary well. I am not aware of
myself. I feel light and airborne. It would be good to give
oneself entirely, so as to leave nothing at all. There are no
happy people: everyone is unhappy, and I am sorry for them
all, profoundly sorry.'[32]

The energy which she generated in such a context reminded
her of the proverbial 'rouble which can't be changed': 'However much you try to spend it you always receive a rouble's
worth change in return.'[33] The rouble formed part of a par-
adoxical, since other-worldly, banking system.

The world thinks, if I gave my love, then I am less well off
in respect of such and such a quantity of love, while if I
were to give the whole of my soul, then I would be left
utterly bankrupt and there would be no point in trying to
save anyone at all. But the laws of spiritual life in this area
are diametrically opposed to material laws. In accordance
with these, whatever of one's spiritual wealth is given away
not only reverts to the donor like the rouble which can't be
changed, but is increased and consolidated. Whoever gives,
receives; whoever impoverishes himself, gains in wealth.[34]

[31] *Mochul'skii*, p. 72.
[32] Ibid., p. 70.
[33] Mother Elizaveta [S. V.] Medvedeva, *o.* (1960).
[34] Mother Maria, 'Tipy religioznoi zhizni' (1937), *MMP*.

Not that the individual should be seen as the ultimate source of such energy and wealth. 'I have been given enormous power (not my own),' she noted, 'and it is crushing me'.[35] 'I am only a voice calling, a sword in someone else's hands.'[36] Even so it is the individual who is obliged 'to quench the sorrows of the world with his own self'.[37] It is a costly, often painful process, but with unforeseen and unsought compensations. Thus she spoke of 'the joys of self-surrender'.[38] And in an unpublished article of 1937 she was to explain:

> Not only do we know the beatitudes, but at this hour, this very minute, surrounded though we are by a dismal and despairing world, we already savour the blessedness they promise whenever – with God's help and by God's will – we deny ourselves, when we muster the strength to lay down our lives for our neighbours, when we seek nothing for ourselves in love.[39]

Less solemnly (and inconsistently) she would sometimes explain the work away exclusively in terms of psychological gains for herself.

> I do not analyse my attitude to people [. . .], but there is one thing which I realize distinctly. I have an inborn sense of compassion. At times it overwhelms me with such force that it dispels all my peace of mind [. . .]. If I have someone to pity, I am prepared to do anything for them. There is no hardship in it, since all the relief comes my way: it is such agony to experience a sense of compassion. It seeks an outlet in care, concern and service in respect of the person you pity.[40]

But whatever the personal motivation, the work could not be conducted by herself alone. Her family were gratifyingly

[35] *Mochul'skii*, p. 70.
[36] *Stikhi* (1949), p. 39.
[37] Ibid., p. 45.
[38] Ibid., loc. cit.
[39] 'Tipy religioznoi zhizni' (1937), *MMP*.
[40] *Manukhina*, p. 141.

loyal to her designs. Her mother acted as churchwarden at Lourmel from the outset. But Gaiana was gone and Iura was as yet too young. In any case it was neither sufficient nor proper to depend entirely on family resources.

One of the first outsiders to join the enterprise was Mother Evdokia Meshcherakova (1895–1977), who had arrived in France from the USSR in 1932. At first no one knew her by her monastic name or title. She kept silent about her secret profession which had taken place in the Crimea five years before. Mother Maria, who invited her to work, and soon to live at villa de Saxe, unwittingly wasted some effort on persuading her to become a nun. Only after some time did Mother Evdokia reveal that the question was long since resolved. For six difficult years she was to work unstintingly at Mother Maria's side. At Lourmel she was to be joined by her sister, Mother Dorofeia Courtin, and by a newly professed nun, Mother Blandina Obolenskaia. At one time it might have seemed that the Metropolitan's hopes were being realized at least in part, and that a new type of monastic community was in the making. But the very fact that it was new, and at the same time unstructured, was to cause misunderstandings, conflict and ultimately schism.

Mother Maria's active type of monasticism found favour with Mother Evdokia. At the same time (and ever more strongly) she felt the need to supplement and undergird it with the *opus Dei* and thereby to distinguish it from mere philanthropy.[41] Initially, at villa de Saxe, there was little opportunity for communal worship. Mother Evdokia was the more delighted when the Metropolitan attached Fr Lev Gillet (1892–1980) to the chapel. Although he was necessarily absent on high days and holy days (at this time he was the rector of the capital's first and only French-speaking Orthodox parish), he was able to institute the frequent, almost daily, celebrations of the Liturgy. This was to be continued at Lourmel, where Fr Lev (firmly committed to a life of poverty) made his home in an unfurnished and rat-infested

[41] Mother Evdokia Meshcherakova, *o.* (1963 and 1967).

outhouse. He was to live there until his departure for London in February 1938.[42]

Mother Evdokia was one of several who invariably attended such services. For her part Mother Maria, keeping to a different time-table or to none, was markedly less often in evidence. Even if she came to one of the weekday services she might stay for only a part of it. There was much that drew her to what Tagore had called the 'lonely dark corner of a temple with doors all shut'. But there was work to be done. A significant part of the morning spent in church might leave the produce from Les Halles unsorted, the midday meal unprepared. In this sphere she had her 'liturgy beyond church bounds [*vnekhramovaia liturgiia*]', a 'liturgy projected from church to world'.[43] Those who commented on her absence from services failed to take into account her insistence that 'in the boring, workaday and sometimes prosaic ascetical rules concerning our attitude to our neighbour's material needs, there is already [or: also] a pledge of possible communion with God'.[44] In its turn, piety at the expense of such communion would aggravate Mother Maria and grieve her. When she learned that Mother Evdokia had been taking a collection in the stable church for the purchase of liturgical texts she was aghast. Could such expenditure be justified in an age of unemployment and distress? 'What hurts me is that even among those closest to me I can feel a barrier in respect of the most basic things', she wrote in her notebook. 'Piety, piety, but where is the love which removes mountains? The further I go, the more I accept that it alone is the measure of things. All the rest is more or less necessary external discipline.'[45]

As time went by it became increasingly more obvious that Mother Evdokia still retained an earlier loyalty to the regulated dedication of conventual life, the life of which the Rus-

[42] Archimandrite Lev Gillet, various personal communications.
[43] Mother Maria, 'Itogi 7-mi let' (1939), *MMP*. See also her 'Mistika chelovekoobshcheniia', *Krug. Al'manakh*, No. 1 [Berlin 1936], p. 158.
[44] *Pravoslavnoe Delo* (1939), p. 38.
[45] MS notebook, *MMP*.

sian revolution had deprived her (the monastery near Gursuf where she had been professed was closed down in 1929, and not one of the Soviet Union's monastic institutions was to be left open a decade later). By contrast Mother Maria was convinced that the same Revolution had at least given émigrés a new (indeed, unprecedented) freedom in church life to experiment, a freedom which it would be dishonest and irresponsible to ignore. 'Our Church was never so free', she said to Mochul'skii. 'Such freedom that it makes your head spin. Our mission is to show that a free Church can work miracles. And if we can bring back to Russia our new spirit – free, creative, daring – our mission will be accomplished. If not, we shall perish ignominiously.'[46] In keeping with such remarks she wrote:

> We can assert that our emigration will justify itself on the religious plane only if it is to be based firmly on genuine religious freedom, if it does not submit to the temptations of contemporary idolatrous religions, if it manages to sustain throughout its wanderings an unsullied faith in man, in his likeness to God, in the ultimate and incomparable value of the human person. We know how in the past religious freedom was trampled down by forces external to Christianity. With almost complete assurance we can say that in Russia any régime whatsoever is going to prepare concentration camps [*Solovki*] to deal with religious freedom. And for this reason we are the more inclined to consider our gift of freedom as something utterly exceptional and providential; we consider it more valuable for us than any earthly prosperity, any external recognition or stability. And we are obliged, in the first place, to be firm and brave in the defence of our Christian freedom against attacks, whether they be motivated by malevolence or by ignorance. In the second place, we are required to be worthy of our freedom, which means that we have to impregnate it with the maximum creative energy, to fire it with

[46] *Mochul'skii*, p. 65. Cf. Mother Maria, 'Pod znamenem nashego vremeni', *Novyi Grad*, No. 12 (1937), pp. 115–22.

the most genuine spiritual zeal, and to transform it into action, into the ceaseless work of love.[47]

Mother Evdokia never ceased to admire Mother Maria's integrity, enthusiasm, energy and power. But with their different personalities it was all the more difficult to reconcile divergences on matters of principle. Apart from which in this 'ecclesiastical Bohemia' (as Mother Evdokia defined it) there was no mother superior to arbitrate between them: the question of precedence was never settled or even discussed. Yet neither partner eventually felt at ease with the other. 'I was afraid of Mother Maria and she was enervated by me', recalled Mother Evdokia later.[48]

The arrival of Archimandrite Kiprian Kern (1889–1960) from Yugoslavia in 1936 and his appointment as resident priest at Lourmel brought not the hoped-for resolution of the problem but aggravation of it. Metropolitan Evlogii had sent for Fr Kiprian in the hope that the latter, by his example, would educate Mother Maria 'in the correct understanding of the monastic vocation'.[49] But it could hardly have been expected that the erudite Fr Kiprian, with his uncompromising piety cast in traditional moulds, and his moody, difficult and demanding personality could be so assimilated by such a community as Lourmel that he might transform it from within rather than disrupt it. 'Our new priest is a nice man,' wrote the perceptive young Iura Skobtsov, 'he is very clever, but he is too severe.'[50]

It was natural and understandable that he should consider it within his rights to guide the other nuns towards a more conventional monastic routine. At the same time it was more difficult to justify the tactlessness with which he repeatedly

[47] *Pravoslavnoe Delo* (1939), pp. 94–5.
[48] Mother Evdokia, *o.* (1963), Cf. the judgement of S. Priestley, who met Mother Maria in 1937: 'Everyone [at Lourmel] respected her very greatly and also feared her, a fear which I shared' (letter to the author, 1974).
[49] *Evlogii*, p. 566.
[50] Letter (in English) of 5 November 1936 to C. Ellison, *MMP*. On Fr Kiprian's character see the obituaries of him in *Vestnik RSKhD/Le Messager* (1960), No. 1, pp. 44–55.

challenged Mother Maria and questioned the foundations on which she strove to build.

The fault was certainly not all on one side. On a number of occasions Mother Maria went out of her way to exasperate Fr Kiprian as if to demonstrate her independence of him and of the tradition which he sought to represent. He was to remain at Lourmel for the best part of three years. But these were years of mutual misunderstanding, tension and bitter (albeit eventually silent) conflict.

Mealtimes in the canteen were particularly oppressive. Fr Kiprian would come down to table in silence, eat in silence and retire in silence. Thus he would demonstrate the 'proper' monastic approach to such activities, while also registering his displeasure at the provision of non-monastic foods for all and sundry. Were not Wednesdays and Fridays almost invariably days of abstinence (not to mention Lenten periods)? He could not be swayed by Mother Maria's counter-argument that hospitality took precedence over fasting: the canteen's homeless clients should be allowed to feel that 'they share their food with us nuns as our guests' rather than as recipients of charity.[51]

Even in his room on the first floor Fr Kiprian was not safe from provocation. Immediately below was located Mother Maria's room, and the animated gatherings which took place there – sometimes well into the night – left him ill at ease. The hum of conversation, punctuated by laughter, would penetrate the well-worn floor boards together with tobacco smoke and link him with a world for which he had little affection, despite (or perhaps because of) his own derivation from it, the world of the intelligentsia. The fact that the participants of the downstairs meetings (people of the calibre of N. A. Berdiaev, G. P. Fedotov, I. I. Fondaminskii or K. V. Mochul'skii)[52] were busy with a creative assessment of

[51] Mother Maria, quoted by S. V. Nosovich, memoir, *MMP*.
[52] The journal *Novyi Grad* served in some degree as a mouthpiece for them. It was edited by I. I. Bunakov [=Fondaminskii] and G. P. Fedotov (14 issues, 1931–9). F. A. Stepun was co-editor until the sixth issue. In addition, members of this circle contributed frequently to Berdiaev's journal *Put'* (61 issues, 1925–40).

some of the world's most acute problems was no comfort to him.

For her part, Mother Maria was sometimes driven to despondency, even (uncharacteristically) to despair by the futility of the confrontation. In May 1939 she was to write:

Three years a guest. And these three years
the loaf from which we cut our bread is one.
The views we have are of the same horizons,
our floors connected by one narrow set of stairs.

Three years I hear those steps above my ceiling.
Three years the house is altogether dumb.
I seriously doubt the wind could sweep it clear.
There's no way out, no victory to be won.

Some sort of cobweb overlays the house,
some sort of dust, some lie. And misery
has left its mark throughout. In my distress
I yearn to end all silences in days to come.

Whose handiwork is this? Whose jest?
Would God tempt us with hate?
My feet are frozen to the spot.
To flee from home! If only I could run.[53]

To flee from home? Already in 1937 she had spoken to Mochul'skii of her intention to give the house at Lourmel over to the other nuns[54] and to set off through France as a wanderer:

It is all clear to me now: either Christianity is fire or there is no such thing. I just want to wander through the world, calling, 'Repent, for the kingdom of God is at hand.' And to accept it if people revile me and say all manner of evil against me.[55]

That same year she wrote: 'Although we are called to spiritual

[53] MS, *MMP*. First published Hackel, *MM* (1980), p. 79.
[54] By now they were four in number: Mother Feodosia Solomianskaia had joined the nuns Evdokia, Dorofeia and Blandina.
[55] *Mochul'skii*, p. 71.

poverty, to folly for Christ's sake, to persecution and vilification, we know this to be the only vocation given by Christ, who made himself of no account and is himself persecuted, vilified and impoverished.'[56] Meanwhile, however (as a chance visitor noted), 'Mother Maria was always surrounded by people as if she was in the middle of a disturbance'[57]: the tensions were considerable, and they badly needed to be resolved.

Mother Evdokia was already searching for alternative premises, where a more regular monastic life might be established. With the support of the Anglican Bishop of Truro (Walter Frere) and the Fellowship of St Alban and St Sergius (of which Bishop Frere and Metropolitan Evlogii were jointly presidents) she visited England to gather funds for this purpose from Anglican convents. But in the event it was Mother Maria who brought matters to a head by asking the others to leave. By the autumn of 1938 Metropolitan Evlogii had helped the nuns to re-establish themselves at Moisenay-le-Grand (Seine et Marne).[58] In the following year Fr Kiprian moved to the Theological Academy, where he was to flourish as a scholar, while also acting eventually as priest of the parish at Clamart. By a resolution of Metropolitan Evlogii, dated 14 September 1939, Archimandrite Kiprian was ('with his own consent') released from his responsibilities as rector of the Pokrov church at Lourmel.[59] So ended this unfortunate episode.

The clash of personalities could be relegated to oblivion. Yet this was also a clash of principles. It was to these principles that Mother Maria was to return in one of her short plays, *Anna*. As is noted in the Soviet *Shorter Literary Encyclo-*

[56] 'Tipy religioznoi zhizni' (1937), *MMP*.
[57] S. Priestley, letter to the author (1974).
[58] *Evlogii*, p. 567. In 1946 the community was to move to Bussy-en-Othe (Yonne), where it has remained to the present day (1981). Mother Evdokia headed the community until her death in 1977. Her obituary is given in *Vestnik RKhD/Le Messager*, No. 122 (1977), pp. 179–84.
[59] *Tserkovnyi vestnik zapadno-evropeiskoi eparkhii* (1939), No. 9–10, p. 6.

pedia, this may be seen as her 'programmatic work',[60] as an apologia for her way of life.

The first act, set in a convent, establishes the conflict between two nuns, Anna and Pavla. Anna is full of concern for the sufferings of the world beyond the convent gates. As Pavla claims,

> Through her the world has broken in
> with all its sores, corruption, blood,
> its passion and disasters.
> Thus everything is darkened, sullied and disturbed.
> If a monastic house is overcome by storms
> where then can peace be sought?

Pavla is convinced that the monastic rule should shield nuns from the outside world. Anna insists that Christianity prompts participation in it:

> We bear the world's cross on our shoulders.

A visiting archimandrite is called upon to judge between them and to restore peace in the community. He decides to send Anna out into the world: she is to serve it and to put her own definition of a monastic as 'manure for the Lord's paradise' to the test. Meanwhile Pavla (after the customary evening meal) follows the community to church. She never misses a service. However difficult some of the liturgical texts may be to understand, her professed aim is to further the salvation of her soul.

Out in the world (Act II) Anna meets a Faust-like wanderer who is on the point of completing three centuries as Satan's subject. During these centuries he had been granted unlimited powers on the one condition that Satan is ultimately to possess his soul. His bargain had allowed him to find a substitute at any stage of the three hundred years prior to his damnation. But despite his offers of power, riches, beauty and perpetual youth, no one – not even prisoners under sentence of death – had ever been persuaded to take his place. Anna

[60] L. N. Chertkov in *Kratkaia Literaturnaia Entsiklopediia* (Moscow 1962–75), iii. 878. The play itself is published in *MM* (1947), pp. 41–73.

1 *Childhood*. Liza Pilenko aged eleven.

2 *Motherhood*. Elizaveta Kuz'mina-Karavaeva with Gaiana and her nursemaid. Sophia Pilenko and her son Dmitrii complete the family group (*c.* 1915).

3 *Exile*. Elizaveta Skobtsova with her children Iura, Nastia and Gaiana, newly arrived in France (1923).

4 *Bereavement*. Nastia Skobtsova in hospital, drawn by her mother (March 1926).

5 *Episcopal support*. Metropolitan Evlogii Georgievskii (1929). A photograph which he gave to Gaiana.

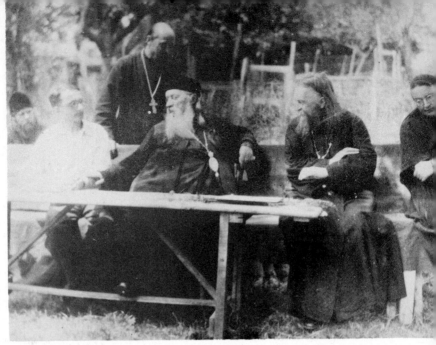

6 *Theological debate*. At a conference of the Russian Student Christian Movement (1934). Metropolitan Evlogii turns to I. V. Morozov (left). To the right: Fr Sergii Bulgakov and Mother Maria.

7 *Service of the needy*. 77 rue de Lourmel (photographed in 1965).

is not persuaded either. None of these blandishments have power over her. But she has power over herself. Of her own free will she undertakes to exchange her life for his. At the cost of her eternal damnation the wanderer is reprieved. He dies repentant and at peace. Anna prepares for torment.

To her astonishment she discovers (Act III) that evil has no power over her. Love and self-sacrifice cannot be contained by hell. Out of love she had accepted the burden of a stranger's evil. By the power of love she had unwittingly overcome it.

In this play Pavla is not condemned outright. It is suggested that her naive pride is at fault as much as her chosen way of life. As Mother Maria wrote in an article of 1937, 'It is impossible to condemn those [. . .] who proceed by alternative ways, which are conventional [. . .], which demand no self-sacrifice, which fail to reveal all the mystery of love. Yet neither is it possible to keep silent about them.'[61] Certainly there can be no doubt as to which of the characters in *Anna* speaks for the author.

Though the setting may be stylized and the plot deliberately unrealistic, it is tempting – it is certainly not difficult – to recognize Mother Maria herself as Anna and to anticipate her progress from her first quiet retreat through the corruption and suffering of the world to her willingly accepted degradation and destruction at Ravensbrück.

---

[61] 'Tipy religioznoi zhizni' (1937), *MMP*.

5

ORTHODOX ACTION

'The more I think, the more I come to the conclusion that my way is correct, that other ways are not for me', she said. 'Correct, but oh how difficult!'[1] Difficult and lonely: 'Whatever happens, in complete isolation and faced in general with lack of understanding, I have to take my own line, accepting it as a spiritual endeavour [*podvig*],' she urged herself in her notebook, 'and not because this is what I want, but because this is what I am required to do. Someone else will complete the work, as for me I must begin without assuming that I shall be the one to complete it.'[2] 'I get very depressed', she admitted at the time when the disputes at Lourmel were at their height. 'I could desist, if only I could be convinced that I stand for a truth which is relative.'[3] In 1937 she marked even Christmas in a minor key:

> How burdensome each step becomes.
> Steeper and lonelier the way.
> They do not prophesy eternal bliss,
> these sounds of every day.[4]

However, as she wrote two years later, 'Unless we engage in intense spiritual endeavours, traverse untrodden paths and sternly dismiss spiritually facile or practically tempting ways, we shall not be able to achieve anything at all.'[5]

To overcome depressions she would throw herself into spring-cleaning, the washing of floors, the painting or paper-

[1] *Mochul'skii*, p. 66 (entry for 1933).
[2] MS notebook (entry for 18 October 1934), *MMP*.
[3] *Mochul'skii*, p. 71 (entry for 1937).
[4] MS (7 January NS 1937), *MMP*; Hackel, *MM* (1980), p. 87.
[5] 'Itogi 7-mi let' (1939), *MMP*.

ing of walls. Physical exhaustion brought a certain peace of mind. Above all it was the manifestation, even the symbol of mortality.

> Tiredness teaches you: desire no more
> commitments, joy or pain.
> For ever lay me down to sleep.
> I pray the Lord my soul to keep.[6]

At times she would even seek to 'grow so tired as to become nothing, to disappear[. . .]'.[7]
But in general she seemed to be tireless. In the words of Mochul'skii,

> She does not recognize the laws of nature, she does not know the meaning of cold, she goes without food or sleep for twenty-four hours at a time, she ignores illness and tiredness, loves danger, knows no fear and hates any form of comfort, whether spiritual or material.[8]

Much of her extraordinary energy was spent on people who were prevented from leading a tolerable life by poverty, alcoholism, mental illness or disease. In them she found her prophets: in them the Son of Man was to be perceived and welcomed.

> I searched for singers and for prophets
> who wait by the ladder to heaven,
> see signs of the mysterious end,
> sing songs beyond our comprehension.

> And I found people who were restless, orphaned, poor,
> drunk, despairing, useless,
> lost whichever way they went,
> homeless, naked, lacking bread.

[6] MS (17 June 1937), *MMP*; Hackel, *MM* (1980), p. 88 (freely translated). A comparable association between sleep and the prospect of death is made in the prayer of St John Damascene which forms part of the daily evening prayers in Orthodox manuals (English tr.: *A Manual of Eastern Orthodox Prayers* [London 1954], p. 18).
[7] *Stikhi* (1949), p. 35.
[8] *Mochul'skii*, p. 67.

There are no prophecies. Only life
continuously acts as prophet.
The end approaches, days grow shorter.
You took a servant's form. Hosanna.[9]

Many of the emigration's 'drunk, despairing, useless' had
drifted to the outskirts of Paris, where derelict slum properties
– then as now – provided the core for shanty settlements.
Mother Maria and her associates would seek them out, provide food and advice, support and consolation. 'Thursday'
schools for the children were set up in various parts: one at
Lourmel, another in rue Jobbé-Duval (XVe), a third in the
industrial region of Montrouge. The school at Montrouge in
its turn paved the way for the establishment of a modest
parish, headed by a dedicated (albeit undervalued) priest,
formerly a pastor of the Reformed Church, Fr Valentin
Bakhst.[10]

But many of the destitute lived a semi-nomadic life. Only
occasionally could they be located. Some at least might find
their way to Les Halles. In all-night cafés like La Grappe
d'Or (rue Courtalon, Ier), homeless people were allowed a
seat until early morning for the price of a glass of wine. No
bedding was provided and, officially, customers were not
allowed to sleep on the floor. But they could sleep with their
heads resting on their forearms, propped against the table.
'I went there sometimes with Mother Maria', wrote Fr Lev
Gillet. 'She used to speak with them and encouraged them to
come to her house, where she gave very cheap meals to the
unemployed.'[11] 'My feeling for them all is maternal', noted
Mother Maria. 'I would like to swaddle them and rock them
to sleep.'[12]

[9] MS, *MMP*; Hackel, *MM* (1980), pp. 88–9; also (but with misreadings)
Stikhi (1949), pp. 40–1.
[10] *Evlogii*, pp. 492–3.
[11] Archimandrite Lev Gillet, letter to the author (1963). According to J.
Chancellor, caution had to be observed in visiting such an establishment:
'It is better not to enter *La Grappe d'Or*, but the door can be pushed open
for a moment or two' (*How to be Happy in Paris* [London 1927], p. 175).
[12] *Mochul'skii*, p. 66.

Among the unemployed she found many who resented the enforced idleness which qualified them for the dole, yet who now feared the freedom and responsibility involved in parting from it.

At least the dole paid for drink, and drink provided an escape. 'My friend died a blessed death. He had his fill of drink throughout the evening, and hardly managed to crawl home to his shack. There he settled down to sleep. Next morning, no answer when we knocked. When we looked in he was already cold. There's bliss for you! Let's drink to such a blissful end.' Savage remarks like this made their impact on Mother Maria: she was to incorporate them into one of her poems.[13] Nevertheless concern for such casualties involved concern for their eternal well-being. Their death might be wretched and her description of it in her pre-war poetry strikingly devoid of religious (=comforting) imagery.[14] Yet the most wretched and sinful (as she repeatedly insisted) would be summoned into the divine presence and even – contrary to all expectations – into authentic and eternal bliss.[15]

Her search for homeless outcasts was not only conducted en route for Les Halles. At times she would disappear for days on end to share in their existence.

For to bring them to one of her establishments for nourishment or even shelter did not necessarily solve their problems. A symbol of the instability and amorality endemic of their situation was provided by a tubercular patient who had been lodged at Noisy. In the quiet of an afternoon, when the nun on duty was having a rest, he took the establishment's two pigs off in a borrowed lorry and was never seen again.[16]

It was not the only occasion when someone took advantage of Mother Maria. But however much bitten, she never grew shy. She preferred to take risks and to make allowances when her trust was abused.

[13] *Stikhi* (1949), p. 82.
[14] *Stikhi* (1937), p. 77.
[15] Ibid., pp. 22, 24, 62.
[16] F. T. Pianov, *o.* (1960).

Thus in 1934 (it was still at villa de Saxe) she offered free keep to a young morphine addict, who almost immediately stole twenty-five francs from Gaiana. There was little doubt as to the culprit. The girl was the talk of the house. Even so, Mother Maria deposited twenty-five francs under a divan. At dinner, with everyone assembled, she announced that she had found the money there: 'You can see how dangerous it is to make accusations without checking first.' The girl burst into tears.[17]

On another occasion, a woman who had pawned her livelihood, a sewing machine, appealed for help. Mother Maria redeemed the machine with funds at her disposal. It was brought to Lourmel and the original owner used it as much as she needed. Eventually she earned sufficient to turn to other work. She passed the machine on to a friend, who also used it freely at Lourmel. But when Mother Maria wondered whether it could not be left there on a permanent basis for yet others to earn something from it her suggestion was met by violent abuse and a blunt refusal. One of Mother Maria's assistants (Sophia Medvedeva) broke down under the assault. Mother Maria comforted her with a cheerful smile: 'If we were doing nothing, there would be no cause to curse us.'[18] 'The odd mistake is no worry', she wrote. 'The only ones to make no mistakes are those who do nothing.'[19]

Her help was often resented even by those who benefited much more substantially from it. Such resentment provided constant reminders of the fact that 'It is not enough to give, we must have a heart that gives. In order to give we must have compassion enough for our gift to be forgiven. For if we give out of duty, if we are charitable only in our actions, the recipient receives humiliation and sorrow and pain together with our gift.'[20] In this connection she quoted St Isaac of Syria:

[17] *Mochul'skii*, p. 68.
[18] Mother Elizaveta [S.V.] Medvedeva, *o.* (1964).
[19] *Pravoslavnoe Delo* (1939), p. 8.
[20] Anthony, Archbishop (subsequently Metropolitan) of Sourozh, sermon (1964).

The person who is genuinely charitable not only gives charity out of his own possessions, but gladly tolerates injustice from others and forgives them. Whoever lays down his soul for his brother acts generously, rather than the person who demonstrates his generosity merely by his gifts.[21]

Furthermore she never lost sight of the fact that her fellow émigrés were not at their best: they have 'suffered enough and are sufficiently distraught for us not to be surprised if even a worthy enterprise encounters substantial obstacles'. Even so, she added, 'I believe we shall succeed, since an enterprise founded on authentic Christian love cannot but succeed.'[22]

Her immediate colleagues sometimes found it difficult to tolerate her tolerance. When she overstepped the bounds of prudence to an untoward degree it was fortunate for her that she had a sober business manager at hand in the person of Fedor Timofeevich Pianov. Pianov's common sense acted as a salutary foil to her enthusiasm, a check on her impetuousness. From the middle of the thirties she was to benefit constantly from the administrative experience which he had gained in the executive of the Russian Student Christian Movement (1923–35). Clash though they might, she learned to appreciate his unambiguous advice and to see beyond his somewhat abrupt manner to his deep-seated concern for the needy, a concern which was expressed more in his tireless work than in his words.

At one stage she urged Pianov to appoint a certain émigré aristocrat as warden of the recently established rest home at Noisy-le-Grand. Pianov interviewed the candidate and duly made the appointment. Some months later Pianov arrived in Noisy from Paris. On his way from the bus stop to the rest home he was hailed by one of the local tradesmen with a query about a substantial sum still owed to him by the man-

---

[21] *Pravoslavnoe Delo* (1939), pp. 35–6. She quotes (and lightly adapts) the text given in the Russian translation of Isaac: *Tvoreniia izhe vo sviatykh ottsa nashego avvy Isaaka Siriianina* [. . .]. *Slova podvizhnicheskiia* (Sergiev Posad 1893), pp. 278–9.

[22] *Novyi Grad*, No. 4 (1932), p. 76.

agement of the home, a matter of 200,000 francs. Pianov was aware of no such debt. He returned immediately to his office in Paris, found the bill in question, which looked as if it had been receipted, travelled once more out to Noisy and confronted the warden with the facts. The man admitted his embezzlement. Pianov contemplated no legal action. However, money was scarce, and this was no way to lose it. Clearly the warden had to be replaced. But when the situation was explained to Mother Maria, she came to an alternative conclusion. In her opinion it was Pianov's behaviour which was improper and inhuman. Fortunately, the home at Noisy was not leased to Mother Maria personally, but to a board of trustees which she chaired. Pianov's fellow trustees were in a position to give him all the support he required.[23]

Even so, Mother Maria was not to be weaned from her ways. Several years later, during the German Occupation, Pianov learned of a mysterious occurrence: the gardener at Noisy had hanged a dog. He came to investigate only to find that there was much more to investigate than this one manifestation of the man's instability. Stores had been disappearing in considerable quantities from the home, and it was the gardener (as it transpired) who had been disposing of them on the capital's black market. Pianov immediately informed Mother Maria and urged that the gardener be dismissed. Once more Pianov found himself classified as inhuman.[24]

He was also to be faced with administrative problems at Lourmel as the result of Mother Maria's generous ways. On one occasion an inspector from the municipal *Bureau de Travail* appeared at his office with a demand for a list of forty members of staff employed at the hostel and canteen. Pianov knew of no such list, still less did he know of such staff. When Mother Maria was summoned she was able to provide an explanation. According to the law, work permits were not issued to the unemployed who were not in possession of an employer's offer of a job. Yet such an offer was usually not forthcoming unless the would-be employee already possessed

[23] F. T. Pianov, *o.* (1964).
[24] Ibid.

56

a work permit: employers could ill afford the time required to negotiate fresh permits. The unemployed were caught in a vicious circle. Mother Maria had decided to break it by issuing an unrestricted number of offers to work at Lourmel, graced with Pianov's official seal. 'The inspectorate was tolerant', noted Pianov: she was not prosecuted. But she was required to give an assurance not to issue further offers or certification of this kind.[25]

In fact, actual staff at Lourmel were few. One of the most committed (and most permanent) was Anatolii Vasil'evich Viskovskii, who worked in the kitchen. This self-effacing, silent man was one of a number of patients (the unfortunate gardener at Noisy was another) who had been released from mental hospitals as the result of Mother Maria's efforts. His devotion to her was unlimited.

It was in the week before Christmas 1938 that Mother Maria, feeling tired and depressed, had set out on her first systematic survey of the mental hospitals which she had known previously only as an occasional visitor. Her aim was to establish how many Russian-speaking patients were confined in them and, more important, how many of them could be discharged. She was away from Paris for five days, travelling (as she always did) without luggage and with minimal funds. She returned astounded to Lourmel. The émigré newspaper *Posledniia Novosti* was soon to carry her account of the three 'difficult and remarkable days' which she had spent in one of the hospitals, the asylum at St Slie.

With one exception (a woman who had been admitted in 1899), all the Russian-speaking patients had arrived at St Slie since the Revolution. Many were victims of either the European or the civil war. The principal psychiatrist assembled them all for Mother Maria to meet. As was explained, these were patients for whom little could be done. Above all the staff needed to communicate with them, yet practically none of the patients spoke any French whatever. Indeed there were some who did not speak at all, others whose speech was

[25] F. T. Pianov, *o.* (1964); MS memoir (1968), *MMP*.

57

limited to a single word. Mother Maria was to encounter one patient who, for seventeen long years, had constantly and with some effort read out the single word 'Lord' from a slate which he always had at hand.

As I entered I expected, naively, that I would be able to address them all with a simple speech. But the sight of my audience left me somewhat dumbfounded. Here, a patient was grimacing, others shouted and gesticulated, some sat completely apathetic. I could only call them out in alphabetical order and interview them one by one.

She was to be particularly struck by one of the patients who seemed to speak for many when he said, 'I am healthy. It's life that's gone mad.'

He came from a small village in Perm', which was eighty kilometres from the nearest railway. It is easy to picture the way of life which he considered normal: the winter snowdrifts, the spring ploughing, and so on. And life had indeed begun to go mad from the first day of his mobilization, from the first day of explosions and collapsing bodies. Then captivity and ignorance of the Russian language among all who surrounded him: was this not life gone mad? There followed a mad life after liberation, the unfamiliar French language, alien food, an alien way of life. He lacked the flexibility to adapt himself to all this, to accept it as normal. It is more than likely that, had he found himself back in his native village when his illness first set in, no trace of his insanity would have remained.

Now, after two whole decades had passed, were there still patients who had not withdrawn beyond recall?

As I spoke to them I made a note of their condition on the list which lay before me, and as each in turn came forward my hopes of finding some who were sane receded further and further. I felt like an examiner who is anxious for his pupils to pass an exam, and who makes every effort to prompt them with the right answers; but they persist in failing and ignore the prompts.

As the result of a day and a half spent in such encounters eight out of fifty-one interviewees were tentatively listed by her as only mildly abnormal, if not altogether sane. She proposed that the medical staff might examine them the following morning.

She herself acted as interpreter. It was a role of which the importance was to be fully demonstrated in the case of one patient. He invariably answered 'Call-up of 1906' when he was asked his age. As the psychiatrist noted, this should be interpreted as a symptom of his illness. The man had allowed a fact with military associations to displace even the memory of his birth date: his mind functioned only within the framework of the war which had caused his condition. But Mother Maria was able to point out that the uneducated Russian would often express his age in terms of his conscription dates. She rephrased the question. How many years had passed since his conscription? What was his actual age now? 'In this case my attempt to salvage the examinee was crowned with success': he provided the correct answers and was ultimately to be pronounced sane.[26]

The discovery of a single sane patient would have been sufficient to justify the enquiry: in the event, three more were to be found. Of this group, one (at the age of sixty) was apprehensive of the outside world and chose to remain at St Slie as the hospital's employee; another required medical (non-psychiatric) treatment before being discharged; two were ready for immediate release. 'I am immeasurably glad at what I have been able to achieve here', wrote Mother Maria to Lourmel. 'Even for three people to be released is already a good thing.'[27]

Her article in *Posledniia Novosti* alerted the émigré community to the disturbing probability that a similar proportion (8%) of Russian-speaking patients – the enquiries had not been limited either to ethnic Russians or to Orthodox Christians – awaited liberation elsewhere. At the same time it emphasized that the needs of the authentic patients also required attention.

[26] Typescript of an article for *Posledniia Novosti* (January 1939), *MMP*.
[27] Letter of 20 December 1938, *MMP*.

I hear their intermittent laughter-tears
and their demented speech.
Though overwhelmed by bitter grief
I want to give my life for each.[28]

There was a widespread response to the article. Almost immediately a committee for aid to Russian mental patients was established, which decided that all the mental hospitals of France should be investigated. In the course of 1939 Mother Maria herself visited seventeen more institutions. Other members of the committee visited a further twelve. Out of two hundred patients, 'no fewer than 15–20 could be restored to normal life'.[29] The work of the committee was noted by the French authorities: on the eve of the war Mother Maria was able to announce that the government had promised 'a centre for four hundred patients'.[30] But the war itself was to put paid to projects such as this.

The medical needs of the emigration were obviously not limited to the psychiatric field. It was fortunate that successive French governments in the course of the thirties had gradually increased the range of rights enjoyed by immigrants in respect of medical care.[31] Some such care was their due so long as they were insured or in possession of a fixed domicile: in particular they might expect free treatment in state hospitals. However, 'the uninsured and those without a fixed residence have great difficulty in obtaining medical assistance.'[32]

Tuberculosis was one of the more common diseases to which émigrés succumbed: Mother Maria was the more aware of it since her own daughter had earlier succumbed to it, while her son was subsequently to contract it when he was barely in his teens. Yet consumptives were particularly disadvantaged since 'the French sanatoria are closed to them for

[28] Draft of a poem, *MMP*.
[29] Mother Maria, 'V mire otverzhennykh' (1940), *MMP*.
[30] Mother Maria, 'Itogi 7-mi let' (1939), *MMP*.
[31] There were notable decrees dated 11 January 1930, 28 October 1933 and 13 January 1937.
[32] *Report of the Nansen International Office for Refugees* [. . .] (Geneva 1935), appendix i, p. 16.

lack of accommodation; and the Russian sanatorium [at Haute Loire] cannot receive them for lack of funds.' Furthermore 'means of assistance are practically entirely lacking for the aged and chronic invalids.'[33]

Many were left to linger and to die in appalling conditions. But even those who might be hospitalized were still affected by lack of sanatoria. They were faced with a premature return to their everyday environment or else an unduly prolonged stay in hospital. In the first case they might suffer a relapse: in the second, reinfection. When Metropolitan Evlogii visited La Rochefoucauld hospital in Paris he met twenty-five Russian TB patients who expressed to him their resentment and despair.

We have been kicking our heels here for years. For years all we see is these walls, and we know there is only one way out for us all – to the cemetery. We have been forgotten. Just occasionally the Red Cross gives us hand-outs of five francs apiece. But that is all. If only some of us, if only one or two of us patients could get into a sanatorium: even that would brighten up our dismal life. Every one of us could then live in hope of success, the way people live in the hope of a win on the National Lottery.[34]

Additional and inexpensive sanatoria were urgently needed. It was the search for likely premises which first brought Mother Maria and Pianov to Noisy-le-Grand. Previous house-hunting expeditions had yielded no results. Here at last they found an imposing, if dilapidated country house in its own grounds. There were lawns for the potential patients' recreation, extensive kitchen gardens for their sustenance, not to mention an orchard of something like four hundred trees. In the language of estate agents, the property was 'ripe for modernization'. But where was the money to be found, not only to rent it, but to make the necessary repairs and installations, to furnish and endow it? These were questions which were immediately posed by Pianov. Mother Maria brushed them aside. There could be no question of

[33] Ibid., loc. cit.
[34] *Evlogii*, p. 486.

by-passing such an opportunity. The sanatorium *must* be established. The minimum funds (if only for the lease) *must* be obtained, and without delay.[35]

Contrary to all expectations it was her impetuosity which was to bear fruit yet once again. Contributions of money and equipment were canvassed in the émigré press. At the same time (and more important) the limited resources of the emigration were soon to be augmented by non-Russian and non-Orthodox supporters based on London, Geneva and New York. Within a matter of months, in the summer of 1935, the new sanatorium was established and Metropolitan Evlogii came to Noisy to preside at its inauguration. He was also to bless the sanatorium's chapel which Mother Maria had converted, with typical panache, from a substantial hen house.[36] It was curious and gratifying for her to learn from Gaiana that she was working in the same field: in the early months of 1936, in the last year of her life, she was occupied in a Moscow architectural workshop with a project for a TB sanatorium.[37]

In the event, the foundation of the Noisy sanatorium proved to be less important in its own right than as a stepping-stone towards a far more comprehensive answer to the problem of émigré tuberculosis. In their work at Noisy, Mother Maria and Fedor Pianov had been assisted by Fr Mikhail Chertkov, an elderly priest, whose particular concern was for the hospitalized Russians of Paris, and who had organized an effective body of volunteer visitors for the sick, based on Lourmel. It was this group of three which now made the necessary arrangements for the Metropolitan to address himself to the Minister of Health, E. Lafont. It was hoped that the Minister, whose wife was Russian, might at least give the problem of Russian TB patients his sympathetic attention. His reply of

[35] F. T. Pianov, *o.* (1964 and 1967).
[36] The chapel (which is still in use) was later to be extended. It was also to be furnished with an unusually fine icon screen by Fr Grigorii Krug (1909–69). Photographs of house and chapel are given in Hackel, *One of Great Price* (1965), p. 85. Photograph of one of the icons in Grigorii Krug, *Mysli ob ikone* (Paris 1978), pp. 97–8.
[37] Letter from Gaiana, 19 March 1937, *MMP*.

September 1936 was indeed (to quote Evlogii) 'unexpectedly favourable'.[38] But few could have envisaged the extent of the reforms to follow. In the following January (and under a new minister) the émigrés were to be suddenly granted the same rights in respect of health care as the remainder of the population.[39] Yet even in anticipation of this decree Lafont was able to assure the Metropolitan that Russian TB patients would be admitted to state sanatoria entirely at the government's expense. It was not long before the Lourmel group was able to have this ruling extended to include also private institutions which received state registration and approval.

Thus within a year of its foundation, Noisy became redundant as a sanatorium. But it was not to remain idle. It was not difficult to turn it into a rest home of a more general kind, up to a third of whose clients were to be received free of charge. During the Occupation it was to be closed and requisitioned by the German authorities, and it was not to resume its functions until 1946. These functions were again to be redefined in 1950, when the house became a home for Russian old age pensioners. Supported by the municipality of Noisy-le-Grand it has remained one to this day (1981). In an upstairs room, crowded with manuscript material and memorabilia connected with the home's founder, her daughter, Sophia Borisovna Pilenko lived out her last years.[40] Even in her late nineties, much of her time was devoted to the transcription of Mother Maria's work: she claimed with some justice that her own handwriting was a marked improvement on her daughter's.[41] Most of this work was completed by the time of her death in her hundredth year (1962).

[38] *Evlogii*, p. 487.
[39] Le ministre de la Santé Publique à MM. les Préfets (affaires générales 97/1937), 13 January 1937. The new minister (H. Sellier) had replaced E. Lafont as the result of a change of government. But his policy in this respect was consistent with that of his predecessor.
[40] A photograph of S. B. Pilenko at Noisy is given in Hackel, *One, of Great Price* (1965), p. 100.
[41] A sample of Mother Maria's handwriting (at its most careful) is given in Hackel, *MM* (1980), plate 9. See also the MS reproduced on plate 11.

The time had come to co-ordinate and consolidate the various enterprises for which Mother Maria was responsible. As early as November 1934 she had discussed 'the organization of Christian social work' with K. V. Mochul'skii and F. T. Pianov.[42] They were fully aware of the Russian Student Christian Movement's 'Committee for Aid to the Unemployed', with considerable achievements to its credit.[43] At the same time they were uneasy in the realization that such work had not played as significant a part as they would have wished in the Movement with which they had been closely connected until now.

Even earlier voices had been raised in the Movement, urging for a more committed programme of Christian social work. Thus in 1928 Fr Lev Gillet (whose own contact with the Russian poor in the south of France had helped to prompt his acceptance of Orthodoxy that year) had written in the Movement's journal:

> Questions of shelter, clothing, sustenance, parental care, health and so forth are more of a burden for the Russian emigration than for any other social group in Europe. Is our Movement to restrict itself to intellectual problems or personal piety, is it to pass by the actual suffering of Russian refugees without pausing, like the priest and levite of the gospel parable? Or, like the Good Samaritan, is it to bend down over the wounded man lying on the road, is it to cleanse his wounds with wine and oil, and to bring him away? We know that hundreds of our brothers not only suffer but die as the result of their material circumstances. Are we really going to do nothing about it?

He proposed that a youth group might be formed within the Movement which would dedicate itself to the service of the deprived: 'In this way a new and special type of religious life

---

[42] *Mochul'skii*, p. 69.
[43] To be renamed 'Committee for Social Aid to Russian émigrés' in 1937. See the survey of its work for 1935 in *Vestnik. Organ tserkovno-obshchestvennoi zhizni* (1937), No. 1–2, pp. 23–4.

might be born, demanding as much self-denial as monastic life, but in conditions which are utterly different.'[44]

Words like this were heeded by few. But it was from these few that the leaders of a new association were to emerge. At first there was no thought of a break with the parent organization (RSCM). In 1932 Mother Maria spoke of continuing her work within it, albeit it on a more independent basis. At most she thought in terms of a new 'missionary society in which both the Diocese [of Western Europe] and the Movement might take part'.[45] Even in June 1935, at a conference of the Movement's secretariat, she spoke only of a 'budding forth of the Movement's organism' prompted by 'the desire for independence in one's work, [yet] in close collaboration with the Movement'.[46] In the event the new association's break with the Movement was to be somewhat sharper and more painful.

Its name, proposed by N. A. Berdiaev, was plain but unambiguous: *Pravoslavnoe Delo* – 'Orthodox Action'. It was to be an expression of Orthodoxy; it was to concern itself with deeds. Among its leading supporters were a philosopher (Berdiaev), a theologian (Bulgakov), a historian (Fedotov), a literary scholar (Mochul'skii) and a poet (Mother Maria, formerly E. Iu. Kuz'mina-Karavaeva). Nonetheless their aim was to set aside theory in favour of practical and unassuming tasks. As early as 1932 Mother Maria had written:

> I am intensely aware at present that any theory, however remarkable, is inevitably less valuable and less needed than any practical work, however unspectacular. The concrete situation is the one whose demands I experience most acutely and before all else.[47]

[44] *Vestnik RSKhD/Le Messager* (1928), No. 11, pp. 14–18. On Lev Gillet's concerns at this time see E. Behr-Sigel, 'The Concelebrant at Clamart: Lev Gillet in the years 1927–8', *Sobornost/ECR* 3:1 (1981), pp. 40–52.
[45] Mother Maria, letter to her family (1932), *MMP*. A photograph of the previous year shows her as a member of the Movement's council (*Vestnik RKhD/Le Messager* [1980], No. 131, p. 359).
[46] Memoir by a participant of the 1935 conference (L. Makarov), *MMP*.
[47] *Novyi Grad*, No. 5 (1932), p. 94.

At the foundation of Orthodox Action she was to paraphrase the same thoughts: 'We are charged with minor tasks and we intend to deal faithfully with that which is minor.'[48]

On 27 September 1935 (it was the festival of the Exaltation of the Cross), the Liturgy at Lourmel was celebrated by Fr Sergii Bulgakov. Orthodox Action was inaugurated at a meeting which followed. It was attended by Metropolitan Evlogii, who gave the new association his blessing. Statutes were discussed and accepted, officers elected. Mother Maria was the obvious choice for the Chair. Her fellow officers were Konstantin Mochul'skii (vice-chairman), Fr Mikhail Chertkov (treasurer) and Fedor Pianov (secretary). The Metropolitan agreed to act as honorary president. Even so the question of whether this was to be a specifically church organization remained open for some time to come. Eventually (in the words of Pianov) 'the general opinion was to the effect that although our honorary president was Metropolitán Evlogii and he gave us the support of his name we should still consider ourselves independent of the church hierarchy – a completely free and independent organization.'[49]

In any case the Russian Orthodox diaspora alone could not hope to finance the association to an adequate degree. As Pianov noted laconically, 'Mother Maria is full of projects, the completion of which depends on funds: these we lack.'[50] Anglican, ecumenical and international agencies were soon to supplement them.

The (Anglican) Russian Clergy and Aid Fund, under its secretary P. E. T. Widdrington, was to make regular if modest contributions from 1937 until the capitulation of France in 1940.[51] Somewhat more substantial aid (c. 400,000 francs per annum) from the American YMCA, channelled through Paul B. Anderson, was able to arrive even beyond that date, and

[48] Ibid., No. 10 (1935), p. 115.
[49] F. T. Pianov, o. (1964).
[50] F. T. Pianov, MS memoir (1968), *MMP*.
[51] See Donald Davis, 'British Aid to Russian Churchmen 1919–1939', *Sobornost/ECR* 2:1 (1980), p. 54. F. T. Pianov spoke in terms of £400 per annum from this source (letter to Joseph Fletcher, 12 November 1947, *MMP*).

was not finally frustrated until the German occupation of Vichy France in November 1942. Through the good offices of Gustav Kullmann, a former YMCA officer who had earlier – throughout the twenties – dealt with Russian émigré affairs and was now (from 1936) a senior staff member of the League of Nations High Commission for Refugees, the League itself began to issue grants from 1936–7.[52]

All this had its importance. Without such support Orthodox Action would have been reduced to a frustratingly modest round of activities. Yet to dwell on the financial or administrative side of its life would be to traduce its ethos. When she reviewed the immediate past of the association on the eve of the Second World War Mother Maria recoiled at the thought that its undertakings were fated merely to develop 'systematically':

In a few decades some history of the Russian emigration might say about us: ORTHODOX ACTION – a powerful charitable and educational organization.[53] It possessed such and such a number of hostels, rest homes, schools, camps, and so on, a well-developed system of hospital work, such and such a number of patients, children, elderly, unemployed and so on. Published such and such a quantity of books and pamphlets. Organized such and such courses. Its accounts were in good order. Its budget was such and such. Everything extremely respectable, possibly even better than in the case of the [Russian] Red Cross or *Zemgor* or even YMCA at their peak, or any other humanitarian, educational or philanthropic organization. Well, if we were really to achieve the most incredible results in this field, I personally feel that I would gain no genuine satisfaction from it. And not only would I resign from such work without

[52] On G. G. Kullmann see N. M. and M. V. Zernov, *Za rubezhom* (Paris 1973), pp. 404–7. At the outset the League of Nations contributed 1,000 Swiss francs (1936–7) and 2,871 Swiss francs (1937–8).
[53] Such a phrase, indeed, was already being used at the time: J. H. Simpson spoke of Orthodox Action as 'a vigorous philanthropic organization' in *The Refugee Problem* (London 1939), p. 316.

any difficulty. I would feel that it had distorted and displaced something that was utterly essential.

Not least of the dangers to be encountered and counteracted is the depersonalization of 'donors' and 'recipients' alike:

> We should make every effort to ensure that each of our initiatives is the common work of all those who stand in need of it, and not [part of] some charitable organization, where some perform charitable works and are accountable for it to their superiors while others receive the charity, make way for those who are next in line, and disappear from view. We must cultivate a communal [*sobornyi*] organism rather than set up a mechanical organization. Our concept of *sobornost'* commits us to this. At the same time we are committed to the personal principle in the sense that absolutely no one can become for us a routine cipher, whose role is to swell statistical tables. I would say that we should not give away a single hunk of bread unless the recipient means something as a person for us.[54]

By no means should this 'require us to ensure that each and every drunk and scoundrel be sentimentally approved by all'.[55] In these matters 'the balance is achieved by care, sobriety and love'.[56] But in their pursuit of this balance the members of Orthodox Action were to be guided by the firm conviction that 'man is God's image and likeness, the temple of the Holy Spirit, the incorruptible icon of God'.[57] And it was this which justified the expenditure of funds or, if need be, lives.

[54] Mother Maria, report to Orthodox Action (1939), *MMP*. A summary of Khomiakov's teaching on *sobornost'* is given by her in E. Skobtsova, *A. Khomiakov* (Paris 1929), pp. 41–2 and 51–4.
[55] Report to Orthodox Action (1939), *MMP*.
[56] Mother Maria, 'Vtoraia zapoved' ', *Pravoslavnoe Delo* (1939), p. 39.
[57] The formulation (by Mother Maria) is based on Gen 1: 26; 1 Cor. 6:19; and 2 Cor. 3:18; quoted in Mochul'skii, p. 70. Cf. *Pravoslavnoe Delo* (1939), p. 40.

6

THE SECOND COMMANDMENT

'We have not gathered together for the theoretical study of social problems in the spirit of Orthodoxy', wrote Mother Maria in 1939. '[. . .] Rather do we seek to link our social thought as closely as possible with life and work. More precisely, we proceed from our work and seek the fullest possible theological interpretation of it.'[1]

Regular gatherings were arranged at Lourmel. Sunday afternoons were set aside for lecturers of such calibre as Nikolai Berdiaev, Sergii Bulgakov, Georgii Fedotov, Il'ia Fondaminskii, Semen Frank, Konstantin Mochul'skii or Boris Vysheslavtsev. An audience of something like sixty people would assemble to hear them. Various weekdays were occupied with wide-ranging 'missionary' courses (which had begun as early as November 1933 at villa de Saxe). Somewhat unexpectedly, there were specialist courses for would-be cantors and readers. In addition to the meetings organized under the auspices of Orthodox Action there were also the regular sessions of Berdiaev's Religious-Philosophical Academy (founded in 1922). Berdiaev had transferred these to Lourmel from the headquarters of the Russian Christian Student Movement (10 Boulevard Montparnasse, XIVe), their previous home for the best part of a decade. None of the founders of Orthodox Action experienced his rift with the Movement as bitterly as Berdiaev (he accused it of fostering right-wing tendencies), and this transfer was its expression and its seal.[2] 'Our close link with the Religious-Philosophical Academy adds considerably to our cultural prestige', noted Mother Maria. On the other hand 'it could be said that ideologically

[1] *Pravoslavnoe Delo* (1939), p. 8.
[2] On the rift see N. Berdiaev, *Samopoznanie* (Paris 1949), pp. 278–9.

we are too clearly defined for adherents of any other ideology to join us or to sympathize with us.'[3]

She was the first to expect and even to welcome reasoned criticism of Orthodox Action. 'As so often happens,' she wrote in 1939, 'external forces – the attacks of opponents, the atmosphere of distrust and suspicion which grew up around Orthodox Action – furthered its maturation.'[4] However, bigoted and spiteful opposition would also provoke her righteous anger and, at times, despondency verging on despair. 'Is my chosen way so futile?' she was to ask in a poem of the early thirties.[5] She was to put the same sort of question to Metropolitan Evlogii one day as they travelled together on the Paris Metro. It was near Bir-Hakeim: the train suddenly emerged from its tunnel, high above the city, from darkness into brilliant light. 'You see – it is the answer to your question', replied Evlogii.[6]

The future might perhaps hold some promise of light. Meanwhile, her ways proved a stumbling block to the pious and respectable churchgoers of the Parisian emigration.[7] Many were affronted by her rejection of conventions which they simplistically equated with Tradition. Was she not a nun? How then could one justify the irregularity of her liturgical life? Her familiarity with the underworld? The shabbiness of her attire? Her smoking (and in public, moreover)? Her cavalier treatment of fasts? Not only is the Rule ignored: even appearances are not maintained. Right-wing émigrés felt that her behaviour smacked of socialism, if not communism. 'Apart from anything else,' wrote Mother Maria, 'for church circles we are too far to the left, for the left we are too church-minded.'[8]

Even some of her close collaborators were inclined to doubt the relevance of her monastic profession to the work she had

[3] 'Itogi 7-mi let' (1939), *MMP*.
[4] *Pravoslavnoe Delo* (1939), p. 5.
[5] MS, *MMP*; *Stikhi* (1949), p. 43.
[6] Archimandrite Lev Gillet, *o.* (1962).
[7] Anthony, Metropolitan of Sourozh, preface to Hackel, *MM* (1980), pp. 13–14.
[8] Address to Orthodox Action (1939), *MMP*.

undertaken. Pianov and Berdiaev had expressed their doubts from the outset. In retrospect Fr Lev Gillet was also to suggest that monasticism added 'nothing essential' to her way of life.[9] At least on the level of inessentials her monastic garb could play a useful role. 'Thanks to my being clothed as a nun, many things are simpler and within my reach', she observed. 'In state establishments it is always easier for a nun to cope with problems, to gain access to the administration or to bypass red tape.'[10]

It is likely that had she been a deaconess she would have encountered less opposition to her work. There would certainly have been less of a gulf between the work and all that was expected of her. But although the possible restoration of the order of deaconesses was under discussion in the Russian Orthodox Church on the eve of the Revolution (and Evlogii, as a young bishop, was then in favour of such a restoration),[11] the question was ultimately to be shelved. A study of the subject which was published at the time concluded that over the centuries the two distinct principles and life styles (cognate, but by no means identical) of deaconess and nun had merged into a single order, the nun's.[12] The fact that Mother Maria was in some sense living the life of one within the framework of the other was no comfort to her critics. Even less easy to accept was her spurning of any framework, rhetoric or custom which might veil uncomfortable truths. In their time the saintly Fools for Christ's sake had sanctified comparable attitudes and procedures. It is not surprising that Mother Maria had a particular devotion for them.[13] The day of one such Fool, St Basil the Blessed (2 August OS), was marked with some solemnity at Lourmel.[14]

[9] Archimandrite Lev Gillet, o. (1962).

[10] *Manukhina*, p. 155.

[11] *Otzyvy eparkhial'nykh arkhiereev po voprosu tserkovnoi reformy* (St Petersburg 1906), i. 84 and iii. 551.

[12] S. V. Troitskii, *Diakonissy v Pravoslavnoi Tserkvi* (St Petersburg 1912).

[13] See her article on the subject, E. Skobtsova, 'O Iurodivykh', *Vestnik RSKhD/Le Messager* (1930), No. 8–9, pp. 3–13.

[14] Mother Maria painted an icon of his life, which is preserved in the chapel at Noisy-le-Grand.

Words spoken by Mother Maria at such meetings which she attended either at Lourmel or elsewhere could not be expected to reach the ears of her distant critics in an undistorted form, if at all. The aid of print was needed. Mother Maria would lock herself away in her room for several hours to write an article or statement. Her manuscripts – difficult to decipher owing to the speed with which she thought and wrote (and rendered the less legible by her extreme short sightedness) – are often entirely covered with lines of words that are regular, compact, confident and firm. An image which was used to describe her poetry could also be applied to her prose. The very script gives an impression of 'volcanic origin': her work emits 'the heat of uncooled lava'.[15]

Even such texts, however firm or fiery, were not bound to reach, still less to sway, her intended audience. But not to write at all would be irresponsible:

> What obligations follow from the gift of freedom which we have been granted? We are beyond the reach of persecution, we can write, speak, work, open schools without bothering about anyone at all. At the same time we have been liberated from age-old traditions. We have no enormous cathedrals, no encrusted gospels or monastery walls. We have lost our environment. Is this an accident? Is this some chance misfortune? Is this perhaps [the natural outcome of] the unfortunate epoch into which we are born? In the context of spiritual life there is no chance, nor are there fortunate or unfortunate epochs. Rather are there signs which we must understand and paths which we must follow. And our calling is a great one, since we are called to freedom.

This being so, old traditions should not remain unchallenged:

> We must be honest and severe to the end. We must liberate the real and authentic even from layers to which we are most accustomed and which we hold most dear. We must deny ourselves any stylizations or aesthetic reformulations

[15] G. A. Raevskii in *Stikhi* (1949), p. 13.

of these essentials. We must scrupulously distinguish Orthodoxy from all its décor and its costumes. In some sense we are called to early Christianity [. . .]. In a word, it is in freedom that we must work as members of the Church. If it becomes necessary for us to enter into conflict, the most surprising discovery will be that the strength of our opponents is negligible [. . .]. But however weak the opposition to be encountered in our own milieu we can and must be tolerant to people while at the same time uncompromisingly intolerant to the ideas which inspire them.

Otherwise excessive tolerance could even lead to betrayal:

In our responsible times [. . .] toleration of antagonistic ideas amounts to treachery in respect of our own faith. We can feed the hungry, comfort the disconsolate, engage in discussions with those from whom we differ, but never and in no respect have we the right to serve a false understanding of Orthodoxy. And, to touch on that which is central and all-important to it, we must not allow Christ to be overshadowed by any regulations, any customs, any traditions, any aesthetic considerations, or even any piety. Ultimately Christ gave us two commandments: on love for God and love for people. There is no need to complicate them, and at times to supplant them, by pedantic rules. As for Christ, he is not testing us at present by our deprivations, by our exile, or by the loss of our accustomed framework. He is testing us – when we find ourselves deprived of our previous living conditions and our way of life, when we are granted our awe-inspiring freedom – to see whether we can find him there, where earlier we had never thought to seek him.

Many will fail to understand this search, deceptively unspectacular and undignified as it may appear. But for those engaged in it there can be no stepping aside:

Freedom calls us to act the Fool for Christ's sake [*iurodstvovat'*], at variance with enemies and even friends, to develop the life of the Church in just that way in which it is most difficult to develop it. And we shall live as Fools, since we know not only the difficulty of this way of life, but also the great bliss of sensing God's hand on our work.[16]

Such freedom is proffered: it needs to be freely and creatively accepted. In an article written at the outbreak of the Second World War, Mother Maria was to contrast the demands made on the military conscript and the Christian:

> We need to understand the meaning of mobilization. If a soldier on being mobilized must leave his well-loved family, his normal work, even his vocation [. . .], if all is taken from the mobilized soldier and all demanded, then our mobilization as Christians must involve personal demands which are in no way milder. At this present moment Christ and the life-giving Spirit make demands on the whole person in all his totality. The difference between this and national mobilization is that the state compels us to mobilize, whereas our faith awaits volunteers. And to my way of thinking the fate of mankind depends on whether such volunteers will come forward, and if they do, on the degree of their self-sacrifice and dedication.[17]

For self-sacrifice is the ultimate application of the Christian's freedom:

> Whether it will prove possible to realize our hopes we do not know. Essentially, this depends on God's will. But apart from God's will, support and grace, demands are also made on each of us: to exert all our strength, to be fearless in the face of even the most daunting task, to generate the spirit of discipline, self-limitation, sacrifice and love, to lay down our lives for our friends, and to follow in Christ's footsteps to the Golgotha appointed for us.[18]

[16] Mother Maria, 'Polozhenie emigratsii', *MMP*; cf. 'Ispytanie svobodoi', *Vestnik. Organ tserkovno-obshchestvennoi zhizni* (1937), No. 1–2, pp. 11–15; and 'Pod znakom nashego vremeni', *Novyi Grad*, No. 12 (1937), pp. 115–22.

[17] 'Prozrenie v voine', *MM* (1947), pp. 146–7.

[18] *Pravoslavnoe Delo* (1939), p. 44.

7

FOREBODINGS

Had Mother Maria chosen to look back on her life at the approach of war in 1939 she might have noted how curiously consistent her progress had been. In one form or another she had cherished the ideals of service and self-sacrifice throughout her childhood, youth and early adulthood as well as in the emigration.

The future founder of churches can already be discerned in the young Liza Pilenko, who took an active interest in the building of her home town's second church (her grandfather and her father were successively its patrons). She contributed the entire contents of her moneybox towards a mural of her patron saint. The restless nun of future years can also be perceived in the seven year old who came to ask her mother whether she might leave home for a convent. Her mother's firm refusal did not deflect her from such plans. Within a year she was back with a request (also to be refused) for an internal passport: she wished to trek with pilgrims from monastery to monastery, from holy place to holy place.[1] Even when she had become a nun her plans to be a pilgrim were not yet abandoned. In 1940 she was to tell Mochul'skii, 'At the first opportunity I shall go to Russia, to the Volga region or somewhere in Siberia. In Moscow I need to spend only a day so as to visit the cemetery and Gaiana's grave. Then in Siberia I shall become a wanderer and missionary among ordinary Russians.'[2]

On the one hand, pilgrimage and mission: on the other, communion with 'ordinary Russians', a latter-day 'going to the people' such as nineteenth-century Russian Populists once

[1] S. B. Pilenko, *o.* (1960) and MS memoir, *MMP*.
[2] *Mochul'skii*, p. 74.

favoured. In childhood the two could coexist. In adolescence, however, the Populist aspect was to come exclusively to the fore. She was to become aware of 'a new hero called the People'.[3] The People, rather than popular religion, were to dominate her thinking for some time.

The change in emphasis was confirmed by her father's premature death in the summer of 1906 at the age of forty-nine. She was fourteen years old and (as she put it) tormented by 'the most vital question of all: do I believe in God? Does God exist?'.

> Then came the answer [. . .]. My father was dead. And the thought in my head was a simple one: 'This death is needed by no one. It is an injustice. That means there is no justice. And if there is no justice there is no just God. Yet if there is no just God, that means that there is no God at all.'
>
> No doubts, no arguments to counter such a deduction. Poor world, in which there is no God, in which death has dominion, poor people, poor me, who has suddenly grown adult since I have uncovered the adults' secret that there is no God, and that the world is ridden with grief, evil and injustice. So ended childhood.[4]

For some years she had to leave the family vineyards near Anapa, the generous sun which shone on them three quarters of the year, the exhilarating Black Sea storms of autumn, which she loved. Together with her family she moved from a newly constructed mansion which was separated only by Pilenko vineyards from Anapa's sands to a modest flat in the northern capital, bleak by contrast, dark, impersonal and misty.

The turbulent events of the preceding year 1905 had helped to accelerate her father's death. They had also caused her to ponder the appropriateness of revolution. Initially her judgement was inhibited and determined by an unusual connection with one of the most influential (and most conservative) figures of the old establishment, Konstantin Petrovich Pobedon-

---

[3] 'Vstrechi s Blokom', p. 265.
[4] Ibid., loc. cit.

ostsev. For twenty-five years (1880–1905) he was the Chief Procurator of the Holy Synod, the administrative head of the Russian Orthodox Church, the trusted mentor of three successive tsars. At court he had long since befriended Liza Pilenko's aristocratic great-aunt, E. A. Iafimovich. Liza's earlier childhood visits to her great-aunt inevitably involved visits to and even from Pobedonostsev.

> Whenever I arrived in Petersburg, [my great-aunt] would write that same day to Pobedonostsev: 'My dear Konstantin Petrovich, Lizan'ka has arrived.' And the next morning he would appear with books and toys, smiling gently, inquiring about my doings, recounting his own [. . .]. In the whole of my childhood I can remember no one who could take such a sincere and careful interest in my childish concerns [. . .]. I loved him dearly and counted him as my genuine *friend*.[5]

By contrast, most sections of the Empire's population (especially the non-Orthodox and the non-Russians) had every reason to hate him. It was thus not altogether inappropriate for Liza to experience the first Revolution of 1905 'as something directed against Pobedonostsev'.[6] But her friendship at first led her to be the 'least tolerant' of her family in its regard.

At the time her father was the director of the renowned botanical gardens near Yalta (Nikitskii Sad) and of the viticultural college attached to them. The political meetings which took place there (with her father's consent) left the thirteen year old Liza bemused.

Away with the Tsar? I was easily able to accept this. A

[5] E. Skobtsova, 'Drug moego detstva', *MMP* (an article which was published in the émigré press sometime in the twenties).
[6] Ibid., *MMP*. Pobedonostsev was to resign office in October 1905. By way of a swan song he had earlier urged the Tsar to 'guard the ideals and principles of power, because without these there is no salvation anywhere, especially in Russia' (appeal of 12 March 1905, quoted in R. F. Byrnes, *Pobedonostsev: His Life and Thought* [Bloomington and London 1968], p. 366).

republic? All power to the people? Again, it all worked out neat and tidy. The Russian Social-Democrat Party? The Party of Socialist-Revolutionaries? It was naturally more difficult for me to make sense of this sort of thing. The one was somehow personified in my mind by the student Zosimov and a lame orator from Yalta, the other by [another] student and his tales about all kinds of exploits and sacrifices. All in all, this revolution with its flurried exaltation was very acceptable, as was socialism. They prompted no objections, while struggle, risk, danger, conspiracy, heroism, and dedicated exploits were nothing if not attractive. On the way to all this stood only one obstacle: Konstantin Petrovich. To be caught up with the Revolution seemed to me to involve a personal act of betrayal [. . .]. That the Russian people were mistaken and that I was in the right was to be deduced from my friendship with Pobedonostsev, from the opportunity to make observations at first hand. But the counter-argument was that after all the whole Russian people could not be mistaken, and I alone aware of the truth. On the theoretical plane the dilemma could not be resolved.[7]

Fortunately 'everything turned out to be much simpler in practice.'[8] Her adolescent doubts were not to torment her for long, and Pobedonostsev ceased to be her criterion in the evaluation of the contemporary scene. On the contrary, when she moved to Petersburg in 1906 her ambition already was to penetrate into genuinely revolutionary groups.

I hated Petersburg. It was difficult to force myself to study [. . .].[9] I was never more frustrated in my aspirations than then. And my spirit longed to engage in heroic feats, even to perish, in order to combat the injustice of the world,

[7] E. Skobtsova, 'Drug moego detstva', *MMP*.
[8] Ibid.
[9] Nevertheless 'Liza Pilenko was an excellent student, for all that she devoted only a minimal proportion of her energy to her work and never paid any particular attention to her successes at grammar school' (Iu. Ia. Moshkovskaia, memoir, *MMP*).

to disperse all this rusty fog and futility [. . .]. I dreamed of meeting real revolutionaries who were daily prepared to lay down their lives for the people. I did meet some students who were petty members of the [S-D] Party, but they were not laying down their lives, merely discussing surplus value, capital and the agrarian problem. This was very disappointing. I could not understand why political economy should be any more fascinating than the accounts which our cook Annushka used to bring to my mother from the bazaar.[10]

In 1910 she was to marry a member of Lenin's Social-Democrat (Bolshevik) Party, Dmitrii Kuz'min-Karavaev (1885–1959). But even this failed to bring her any closer to 'real revolutionaries'. Admittedly, her husband had spent a short time in prison three years earlier for his political activities: as a courier he had helped to link the party cells of Petersburg with those of Finland.[11] However his days in the Party (which he had joined as a student in 1905) were now numbered. He had gravitated towards the intellectual and artistic circles of the capital; he delighted in his new reputation as decadent and aesthete.

Kuz'min-Karavaev's young wife was also plunged into the life of the artistic élite. For a time (as she noted later) 'Petersburg made a conquest of me'. A focal point and symbol of this Petersburg was Viacheslav Ivanov's fifth floor flat, 'the Tower', overlooking the seat of the Duma in the Taurid Palace. The proximity of the two talking-shops to one another was coincidental: their agendas had little in common.

Indeed, the contrast between them only served to emphasise the appropriateness of Berdiaev's designation of Ivanov's flat as an ivory tower in the fullest sense of the term.[12] The writers, composers, designers and philosophers who would meet here determined the character of Russia's 'silver age'.

[10] 'Vstrechi s Blokom', pp. 265–6.
[11] D. V. Kuz'min-Karavaev, autobiographical memoir (in the custody of Fr Paul Mailleux, Rome).
[12] N. Berdyaev, *Dream and Reality* (London 1950), p. 161.

Meetings began late and ended only after dawn. The brilliant, endless and inconclusive discussions initially fascinated Liza Kuz'mina-Karavaeva. Together with the meetings of the newly formed Poets' Guild,[13] which not infrequently met at the Kuz'min-Karavaevs' prosperous flat in Manezh Square, and which assembled such young writers as Akhmatova, Gumilev and Mandel'shtam, it provided a welcome substitute for her university studies on the Bestuzhev Courses for Women: indeed, she failed to return to these after her first year,[14] when the Courses were in any case suspended for a time as the result of political unrest. But at the same time there was something disturbing and disreputable, if not obscene, about the isolation of the Tower's discussions from the people.

> We lived in the middle of a vast country as if on an uninhabited island. Russia was illiterate, whereas in our milieu was concentrated all the culture of the world: the Greeks were quoted by heart, we welcomed the French symbolists, we thought of Scandinavian literature as our own, we were familiar with the philosophy, theology, poetry and history of the whole wide world, in this sense we were citizens of the universe, the keepers of mankind's cultural museum. This was Rome in the time of its decline [. . .]. We played out the last act of the tragedy concerned with the rift between the intelligentsia and the people. Beyond us

[13] The Guild consisted of fifteen members. Anna Akhmatova acted as its convenor. Several volumes of poetry were published under its auspices, including Akhmatova's first collection, *Vecher* (1912) and Liza's own *Skifskie cherepki* (1912). The Guild was to be overshadowed and displaced by the Acmeist group which soon grew up out of it. See Amanda Haight, *Anna Akhmatova* (New York and London 1976), pp. 18–19.

[14] Archives of the Bestuzhev Courses, *Gosudarstvennyi Istoricheskii Arkhiv Leningradskoi oblasti (GIALO)*, f. 113. Later she was to take the unusual step of following the courses at the St Petersburg Theological Academy. She could not be admitted officially to this male institution (and no record of her studies is preserved there), but she studied the course materials at home and those members of the faculty who proved willing to examine her were able to give her the highest grades (S. B. Pilenko in *Stikhi* [1949], p. 11).

80

stretched out the Russian Empire's snowy desert, a country in fetters: it was as ignorant of our delights as of our anguish, while its own delights and anguish had no effect on us.

After the events of 1905 it was all the more clear that revolution might bring down the curtain on this final act:

So everybody stood for revolution; the most responsible utterances were made on the subject. Yet they left me more disenchanted with ourselves than ever before. For no one, positively no one was prepared to die for it. Moreover, if they were to learn that people do die for it, they would have evaluated this too somehow, they would have approved or disapproved, they would have understood it at its highest level and discussed it at the top of their voices – until the breakfast-time fried eggs were served. And they would completely fail to understand that to die for the revolution means to feel a real rope round your neck, to leave life behind for good on just such a grey and drowsy morning, physically and in actual fact to accept death. And I pitied the revolutionaries because they die, whereas we can only discuss their deaths eruditely and on a lofty plane.[15]

Religion was treated in a comparable fashion. Even its proponents seemed to distance themselves from it and thus diminish its role. At the Tower the basic assertion was 'We believe, believe, believe':

But it always seemed as if mention of Sophia the Wisdom of God, references to Solov'ev, belief in God-Manhood might be one thing, while the values of church life itself were considerably more comprehensible and more accessible to any old beggar woman, hard at her Sunday prostrations in church. The main thing for this kind of life was lost: 'Whosoever shall not receive the kingdom of God as a little child shall not enter it.' There was nothing childlike

[15] 'Vstrechi s Blokom', p. 268.

there, nor could there be, there was only the wisdom of old people who had mastered everything and for whom everything had grown cold. And church life had joined the ranks of cultural values. It was carefully studied and stored away in the common treasury of cultural values. Thus there was everything except faith, faith in anything whatsoever: there was only a firm will to acquire faith.[16]

Liza Kuz'mina-Karavaeva ('thirsting for some kind of spiritual feat and speaking of this with sorrow and with pain' at the Tower)[17] could find no solace in such a barren substitute for faith. The beggar woman alone, in all her simplicity, pointed the way to something more authentic.

Gradually a separation takes place. Christ, as yet unrecognised, becomes ever more familiar. The line of division continually deepens. On the one hand Petersburg, Viacheslav's Tower, even culture, fog, urban life, reaction. On the other, the vast, wise, silent and uncorrupted people, the dying revolution [. . .], and in addition – Christ. Christ belongs to us. . . . But who is this 'us'? Am I really where he is? Am I not rather surrounded by irresponsible words which I am now beginning to see as insulting, as blasphemous, as poisonous in the extreme? I must flee, I must liberate myself.[18]

'I must flee': as she may not have remembered at the time she had already been encouraged to think in such terms some years before. The occasion was her first meeting, at the age of sixteen, with the person who was to prove a major influence in her life during much of the succeeding decade, the poet Aleksandr Blok (1880–1921). After their first meeting (Liza had called on him unannounced at his flat) Blok had apparently written to her, 'If it is not too late, then flee from us, who are dying.'[19] Even if she could not hope to merge with

---

[16] Iurii Danilov [=E. Iu. Skobtsova], 'Poslednie Rimliane', *Volia Rossii* (1924), No. 18–19, p. 109.

[17] A. I. Deich, 'Arabeski vremeni', *Zvezda*, 1968, No. 12, p. 199.

[18] 'Vstrechi s Blokom', p. 268.

[19] Letter of February 1908, quoted in 'Vstrechi s Blokom', p. 267.

'the people' elsewhere, she might at least be better placed to meet a person of due simplicity and integrity with whom to fall in love: such was the burden of the poem which he enclosed with the letter. It contains an evocative portrait of the young Liza Pilenko, already concerned with ultimate problems and sombre beyond her years. Unfortunately, Blok's teasing (and in her estimation patronizing) tone was to catch her on the quick: no sooner had she read the poem than she tore it up. No doubt she had cause to regret this four years later when she joined Osip Mandel'shtam and two other friends (Vasilii Gippius and Vladimir Piast) in informing Blok that they had lightheartedly elected him 'king of Russian poets'.[20]

> When you come into my life
> so vital
> so beautiful
> yet so tormented
> speaking only of sad things
> thinking of death
> loving no one
> and scornful of your own beauty
> well
> would I distress you?
>
> Far from it.
> After all I am no rapist
> nor am I devious or proud
> though I know a great deal
> am far too concerned with myself
> have always thought too much.
> But then I am a writer
> someone who gives names to things
> and deprives living flowers of their scent.
>
> However much you may speak of sad things
> however much ponder ends and beginnings

[20] TsGALI, f. 50, op. 1, ed. khr. 375, f. 14. See V. N. Orlov *et al.*, ed., *Aleksandr Blok. Perepiska. Annotirovannyi katalog*, vol. 2 (Moscow 1979), pp. 377–8.

for all that I venture to think
you are only fifteen.
And therefore I wish
you could fall in love with someone straightforward
a man who loves earth and sky
more than rhymed and unrhymed
talk of earth and sky.

Truly I would be glad for you
since only someone in love
has the right to be called human.[21]

Her first husband did not fit the prescription given in the last few lines. She married him 'somehow unexpectedly',[22] 'more for pity than for love, as she herself would say later'.[23] On the wedding day itself Iu. Ia. Moshkovskaia was to note that 'Liza had created him in her own imagination or maybe wanted to save him from some kind of "abyss" '.[24] Undue dependence on alcohol probably helped to determine the nature of this abyss.[25] In any case the marriage was not to last. By the time Liza had finally decided to break with Petersburg at the beginning of 1913 – she had already spent the summer of 1912 in the south – she had also learned to accept that husband and wife should go their separate ways. They were to be divorced before the end of 1916. Neither could have suspected that their respective convictions were eventually to bring each of them to some form of Christian service. In his case, conversion to Catholicism (Moscow 1920) was to lead, in the emigration, to membership of the Society of Jesus and ordination to the priesthood.

When she spoke to Blok on the eve of her definitive departure for the south, Liza referred to a hankering for 'the earth'.

[21] Aleksandr Blok, *Sobranie sochinenii v vos'mi tomakh* (Moscow-Leningrad 1960–3), ii. 288–9. Blok is mistaken about her age: in her memoir 'Vstrechi s Blokom' she herself was to reduce it by yet one more year (p. 267). But she was born in December 1891, and the visit took place in January or February 1908.

[22] Mother Maria, quoted in *Mochul'skii*, p. 66.

[23] Iu. V. Pilenko, letter to the author (1976).

[24] Iu. Ia. Moshkovskaia, memoir, *MMP*.

[25] Mother Elizaveta [S. V.] Medvedeva, *o.* (1964).

The earth seemed to offer new perspectives, a new freedom. 'I have grown somehow closer to the earth', she was to write to Blok as early as November that same year. 'Moreover I have once more come to love someone, and this is a genuine love.'[26] The object of her love, as if in accordance with Blok's prescription, was indeed ' a simple and straightfoward man, a hunter, [the type of] Hamsun's Captain Glan', noted a friend who visited her in the summer of 1915.[27] But no more detailed description of him has been preserved, and even his name is lost. There is all the more cause to regret this since, although he was to vanish from Liza's life during the last years of the Great War, there seems no reason to doubt that he was the father of Gaiana.[28] Gaiana, who was born 18 October 1913, took the surname Kuz'mina-Karavaeva; but the name identified her with her mother, rather than with her mother's estranged husband. However there was nothing ambiguous about her unusual (Greek) first name. 'I have called her Gaiana, the earthly one', explained Liza in a letter to Blok.[29]

Proximity to the earth involved proximity to the people. This in turn prompted a renewed interest in their religion, an interest which was to be reinforced and intensified by the outbreak of war. For a time she was unobtrusively to resort to medieval modes of asceticism and wore a belt of lead.

I buy a thick lead pipe, quite a heavy one. I flatten it with a hammer and sew it into a rag. All this in order to acquire Christ. To compel him to reveal himself. To help me, no simply to remind me that he exists. And my war effort is limited to [the reading of] saints' lives, to the lead pipe, to

[26] TsGALI, f. 55, op. 1, ed. khr. 299, ff. 4–7.
[27] A. A. Afanas'eva, quoted by Iu. Ia. Moshkovskaia, memoir, *MMP*. The reference is to the Lieutenant (rather than Captain) Glan of Hamsun's story, 'Pan' (1894). A Russian translation of it had recently been published in Knut Gamsun, *Polnoe sobranie sochinenii* (Moscow 1910), i. 47–138.
[28] Letter of E. Iu. Kuz'mina-Karavaeva to Blok (late November 1913), TsGALI, f. 55, op. 1, ed. khr. 299, ff. 4–7.
[29] Ibid.

persistent, intense, if fruitless prayer on the cold floor. This is necessary for something, for the war, for Russia, for my beloved people. . . . The people's only need is Christ – this I know.[30]

Such a conviction prompted ascetic exercises; it also demanded to be expressed. By the middle years of the war Liza was beginning to sense that she had some kind of prophetic role to play. As she wrote to Blok in July 1916, her lot was to brave the enemy's arrows and 'to proclaim the simple word of God'.[31]

Not that she could expect such a proclamation to sway Blok himself. Although he seems to have appreciated her concern for his welfare and had earlier asked her to pass by beneath his windows 'almost every day' to give him the assurance that 'someone is guarding and sheltering me',[32] her insistent talk on questions of human destiny tended to enervate him. On a visit to Petrograd in 1916 she subjected him to such talk into the early hours of 14 March. Although their meeting lasted until nearly 5 a.m., this was probably not the only reason why Blok concluded his notebook record of it with the remark, 'I am very tired'.[33] For her part, in a poem for her second collection *Ruf'* (which was published that year), she acknowledged that he was not yet ready to heed 'the sacred message'.[34]

However, the message was not addressed to Blok alone. In the lyrical preface to *Ruf'* its author publicly proclaimed her vocation. In the portentous manner of her day, but in all sincerity, she described herself as a visionary. For all its manifest limitations it is a remarkably perceptive document. It is of interest not only for its assessment of her past, but also for its tentative delineation of her future.

[30] Quoted by S. B. Pilenko, MS memoir, *MMP*; also in *Stikhi* (1949), p. 11.
[31] TsGALI, f. 55, op. 1, ed. khr. 299, ff. 21–2.
[32] 'Vstrechi s Blokom', p. 275.
[33] Aleksandr Blok, *Zapisnye knizhki 1901–21* (Moscow 1965), pp. 290–1.
[34] *Ruf'* (1916), p. 60. On this poem see the remarks of D. E. Maksimov, 'Vstrechi s Blokom', p. 262.

Necessity caused me to ascend the heights. Someone with a destiny does not know why, but is granted a different kind of knowledge: it must be thus.

Leaving the hills and valley below, I saw the limits, and my faith merged with knowledge because I was able to count how many hills separate me from them, and from above could trace all the bends of the road which leads to them [. . .].

Some will, which is unknown to me, determined that I should descend once more into the valleys. As a pilgrim I move towards the sunrise. The mystery which drew me from the heights has been revealed to me: 'unless a grain of wheat falls into the earth and dies, it remains alone; but if it dies it bears much fruit.' I have ceased to see in order to feel my way, so as not only to measure the route by rational means but to traverse it slowly and with love [. . .].

If it is given to me to read the pages of that which has not yet come to pass, if the memory of that which was and is has not prevented me from remembering the number of hills or bends in the road, I yet say in all humility: at present my difficult aim is to ascend the first of the foothills; from these I shall see how the sun rises between the hills; although perhaps it will not be for me to see it rise from beyond the earth's perimeter, from the dark and impenetrable depths. It is probable that I, like many others, will die without having attained the limits, which I perceived from the heights. But they are close, these limits, they are close.

My few companions, who looked together with me or simply believed in my visions, I use a new language with which to remember you; and you shall recognize me in new clothing; we are not destined to part.

And Thou, who hast given me my destiny and hidden the obvious in order to illumine my mind with the mysterious, do not leave me in the course of the earthly sunset, and do not blind my sight which has gained vision by thy will.[35]

---

[35] *Ruf* (1916), pp. 5–6.

As if to confirm and develop such thoughts she wrote to Blok in September 1916, 'It is particularly difficult to realize that each person is only potentially a messenger of God, whereas to realize this potential, it is necessary to proceed via the most prosaic and determined work. And it seems to me that the aim should be to achieve this, for a combination of factors is imminent which will give absolute assurance in faith and fulness of life. Then the law given by God will merge with the law of human life.'[36]

At the beginning of the same letter she remarked, 'My favourite autumn stillness is about to begin and everything that happened in the course of the year is being counted up.' But this was to be the final stillness on the eve of the turbulent events of 1917, when everything inherited over the centuries was to be counted up, assessed and for the most part cast aside. Had she not written, 'Time stands still before disaster'?[37]

For the moment, however, she busied herself with the management of the family estate near Anapa, particularly with the grape harvest, thus allowing herself to be distracted from what she called 'the real'. 'I bustle around for days on end, as if life ought to pass that way', she wrote to Blok in August. '[. . .] Yet it is all more ephemeral than the most forgotten dream.'[38] 'Life goes on pointlessly,' she continued two months later, 'and all life's valuables seem like some sort of bric-à-brac. I know very well and I constantly remember that they only provide a veneer for the real. But if I have earthly eyes, they want to see what is accessible to them, while my earthly ears have to hear that which is earthly. So that while I know of that other and although I knew it, I could not perceive it here.'[39] She returned to the same thoughts in November: 'Side by side with the quiet all sorts of clumsy business goes on: I am mortgaging the estate, buying a windmill, and I am in an

[36] TsGALI, f. 55, op. 1, ed. khr. 299, ff. 25–6. Wrongly dated by the sender 5. xi [rather than ix] 1916.
[37] *Ruf'* (1916), p. 51.
[38] TsGALI, f. 55, op. 1, ed. khr. 299, ff. 23–4.
[39] Ibid., ff. 27–8.

endless flurry. The stupid thing is that all this nonsense is described by the verb "to live". Whereas life proceeds on an altogether different plane and has no need for all this fuss. In it everything is quiet and solemn.'[40] To a relative who visited her in the spring of 1917 she seemed to be 'distracted by something, burdened and somehow disorientated'.[41] But new responsibilities were soon to put an end to her petty concerns and to dispel her dissatisfaction. If there had been a tendency to dally with quietism, no trace of it was to remain.

By way of neo-Populist service (at last that service of the people for which she had idly yearned ten years before) she became convinced as never before of the interrelatedness of the two biblical commandments (Matt. 22: 37–40). 'There can be no question but that a Christian is called to social work', she was to write later:

> He is called to organize the personal life of working people, to provide for the aged, to build hospitals, to care for children, to combat exploitation, injustice, need and lawlessness [. . .]. The ascetical rules are simple in this respect, they make no allowance [. . .] for flights of mysticism, they often limit themselves merely to everyday tasks and responsibilities.[42]

Such tasks and responsibilities were to fill her life in the months which followed the social and political upheavals of 1917.

Her Populist sympathies made it natural for her to join the ill-fated Socialist-Revolutionary (S-R) Party, a party that commanded a deceptively large following during most of 1917 despite the vacillations in its leadership and programme.[43] In the early summer of 1917 she was to attend the party's Third Congress in Moscow as a delegate from Novorossiisk. After

[40] Ibid., f. 29.
[41] Iu. V. Pilenko, letter to the author (1976).
[42] *Pravoslavnoe Delo* (1939), pp. 37–8.
[43] On the S-R Party see O. H. Radkey, *The Agrarian Foes of Bolshevism* (New York and London 1958) and *The Sickle under the Hammer* (New York and London 1963).

the Bolshevik coup d'état she was to support those sections of the party (the majority) who did not align themselves with the new administration in the early months of Bolshevik rule. Although there seems to be no substance in the legend that she once had plans to assassinate Trotsky,[44] there is no doubt that she repeatedly courted danger in 1918 in the course of her conspiratorial activities.

But many of her everyday tasks and responsibilities were undertaken in her family's home town of Anapa. Towards the end of February 1918 she was elected its deputy mayor. With the precipitate resignation of the mayor (Morev) she was required to become acting mayor almost immediately after her election. 'At my own risk I had to work out a line of conduct', she wrote afterwards:

> My main tasks were to safeguard the town's cultural ameni-ties from complete destruction; to ensure that life should be as normal as possible for the citizens; and in extreme cases to defend them from the firing squad, 'ducking' in the sea or similar hazards. These tasks were daunting enough and they sometimes gave rise to impossible situations. In the background there was always everyday life with its everyday problems, the quantity of which gradually de-creased, admittedly, as the Bolsheviks gained ever firmer control and progressively fewer people turned to us.

However, she soon established an easy relationship with the Bolshevik chairman of the local soviet, Protapov.

> My situation was sufficiently secure and I could achieve a good deal mainly because of my being a woman. I feel that this was because the very fact of having a female mayor was seen by the Bolshevik-minded masses as something so obviously revolutionary, as something which involved so firm a break with the customs of the old régime, that from

---

[44] For an unduly credulous acceptance of the legend see T. Stratton Smith, *The Rebel Nun* (London 1965), pp. 66–8. An earlier mention of it is made in Donald A. Lowrie, *Rebellious Prophet: A Life of Nicolai Berdyaev* (London 1960), p. 210.

a Bolshevik point of view this (within certain limits) was sufficient to justify my counterrevolutionary speeches. Therefore they were obliged to take me into account. At the same time there was a great deal that might be tolerated from me which the Bolsheviks would not have tolerated from a single male [. . .]. Finally, a third factor in determining their attitude to me was their conviction that I was sufficiently daring [. . .]. Undoubtedly that is how it may have looked, for that was the only way to get any work done. If, as the result of some dispute with the soviet I felt that my arrest might be in the offing I would declare, 'I'll get you to arrest me yet'. At which Protapov, hot-blooded and romantic that he was, would shout, 'Never! That would imply that we are afraid of you.'[45]

There was certainly no cause to doubt her daring. During her term of office and as the result of her direct interventions, hospitals and schools were protected from pillage. On one memorable occasion she was to safeguard the municipal funds from a band of anarchist sailors (delegates, so they claimed, of the Black Sea fleet) who descended on the town with a demand for protection money, a 'contribution' of twenty thousand roubles. Protapov lacked the confidence to refuse them outright and called a public meeting to determine whether the money should be paid. The question was put to the meeting but received in silence. Only the acting mayor was prepared to disregard Protapov's caution ('Go easy, don't mistake them for us, they've got no inhibitions') and to make a stand. Her forthright declaration, 'I am in charge of this town, and not a kopeck do you get', amused and impressed the sailors. It also swayed the meeting. When it came to a vote, she obtained almost unanimous support. No money was surrendered. 'Curiously enough, the sailors guffawed.'[46]

But Protapov was right: it was dangerous to treat them lightly. They were due to embark the following morning. To

[45] E. Iu. Skobtsova, 'Kak ia byla gorodskim golovoi' (1923), author's typescript, in the papers of I. V. Morozov (Paris).
[46] Ibid.

deflect them from any possible reprisals she decided to take them on a lengthy nocturnal tour of the town and its surroundings. An elderly citizen of Anapa acted as her barely convincing bodyguard. She returned home in the early hours, 'thoroughly exhausted, yet radiant in the knowledge that she had been able to sway the sailors. They had killed no one and had promised to kill no one at Anapa.' However, as her mother added, 'this was a promise which they failed to keep. They took two men away with them, a schoolmaster and the chief of police. When they had sailed out of town they drowned them at sea.'[47]

Liza felt that she was somehow responsible for their fate and considered abandoning her work. When some of Protapov's men – afraid of being brought to justice for plunder – murdered their leader, her decision was taken. Without Protapov's stabilizing influence the precarious status quo in Anapa was in any case threatened and her executive powers correspondingly diminished. After the funeral, towards the end of April 1918, Liza left Anapa once more for Moscow, where she busied herself with S-R party affairs. Meanwhile, civil war had broken out in earnest. The ill-organized factions of the once prominent and promising S-R party were fighting a losing battle for survival on one side of the battle line while incongruously collaborating with reactionary forces on the other.

Liza returned to the south in October as a companion and cover for Evgenia Ratner, representative of the S-R Central Committee in the south-east. They narrowly escaped death en route. A Bolshevik sailor, who had taken charge of the train on which they travelled, decided on the random execution of passengers when he learned that Ukrainian nationalist troops were approaching. Liza insisted that the sailor should first send a telegram to Moscow so that Nadezhda Krupskaia, Lenin's wife, should be informed. Its first sentence, 'Tell Krupskaia I am about to be shot', was enough to convince the sailor that he should desist. Not only did her

[47] S. B. Pilenko, MS memoir, *MMP*.

bluff safeguard their lives: they were not even searched. In fact, the S-R documents which the two of them carried would have sufficed to provoke or even 'justify' their execution, while their discovery would also have put other lives in danger.

In the event, Evgenia Ratner's freedom was short-lived. She was to be one of the defendants at the Moscow show trial of S-R Central Committee members in 1922. After a spirited defence, she was to be sentenced to death.[48] However the original sentence was subsequently suspended both for her and for her co-defendants subject to the 'good behaviour' of their fellow party members and she was to survive in penal exile until 1932.

Liza herself was to be arrested immediately on her return to Anapa. The town had been occupied by the White 'Volunteer' Army in August, and 'everything that determined my anti-Bolshevik work in Soviet Russia seemed on this side of the front almost to be Bolshevism or at any rate, from the Volunteer point of view, something criminal and reprehensible.'[49]

According to the local Kuban government's ill-formulated legislation (which was in any case frequently ignored by the Volunteer Army) it was not altogether clear what penalty she could expect if she were to be found guilty under the relevant article of 'Order No. 10': the prescribed penalties ranged from a fine of three roubles to death. There were many who expected the latter, and one officer in particular who took pleasure in telling her so as she awaited the trial in her cell. When it transpired after six weeks that the trial was to be delayed until 2 March 1919 she was released on bail. She was able to use the respite in helping the families of fellow prisoners who were less fortunately placed.

On the day of the trial she learned that one of the principal witnesses for the prosecution was a man with scores to settle: Dr Budzinskii, formerly mayor and, until the Revolution, virtual dictator of Anapa. Under Liza's administration Bud-

[48] *Pravda*, 7 July 1922.
[49] E. Iu. Skobtsova, 'Kak ia byla gorodskim golovoi' (1923), author's typescript (Paris).

zinskii's three profitable but appallingly run sanatoria had been placed under municipal control, and he had never ceased to resent his disgrace. It was only with difficulty that she was able to convince the court – the Ekaterinodar area military tribunal – that he was manipulating the evidence against her. Thanks to the unexpected intervention of a recent acquaintance, the influential Daniil Skobtsov (1884–1968), she was merely to receive a token sentence of two months' imprisonment, which was in any case suspended.[50] No one could have foreseen that the former schoolmaster who thus acted as her patron was soon to play a different role in her life as suitor and second husband.

The tide of the civil war was soon to sweep her away from Anapa. In any case she no longer had a clearly defined role to play in its life. In retrospect she was able to reflect appreciatively that in a small town like this 'nothing can ultimately overshadow the individual human being':

> And since my basic aim was to defend the individual and since I put aside all other considerations in pursuit of this one aim, I was able to discern the individual even among party and ideological foes.[51]

In the harsh setting of the civil war this was in itself exceptional. But it could hardly compensate for the fact that, in marked contrast to her youthful aspirations to serve the people, her role in Anapa had been reduced to that of an occasional arbitrator in a dispute which was entirely beyond her control. Far from improving the lot of her constituents, she barely succeeded in helping to safeguard something of what they already possessed.

Her family house in Anapa no longer stands. It was probably destroyed in 1942–3 when the town suffered devastation at the hands of the German invaders. At almost the same time, in February 1943, the Nazi security police were to arrest

[50] D. E. Skobtsov, *o.* (1964), communicated by F. T. Pianov.
[51] E. Iu. Skobtsova, 'Kak ia byla gorodskim golovoi' (1923), author's typescript (Paris).

Anapa's former acting mayor in Paris and to deport her to Germany, there to face a martyr's death.

Of this her fate there are hints and premonitions even in the poems of the Anapa period. In *Ruf*, published in 1916, she had written:

> When I expected nothing of the sort
> a blinding flash lit up my lonely path.
> I waited for some voice to answer.
> There's no such voice: I know it now.
> And yet the times are drawing to a close.
>
> Quiet echo of eternal words,
> green mother's silent and mysterious calls.
> As Daniel in the lion's den
> my spirit is prepared for pain.
> The lions are ready to submit.[52]

Similar thoughts are expressed even more clearly in another poem of the same collection, which concludes:

> The blood of martyrs flowered once
> on this infertile earth.
> A hungry lion licked their wounds
> and they went forward to their torture freely
> as by God's grace shall we as well.[53]

In a third poem this progress is explicitly depicted as the bearing of a cross:

> As I denied him for the final time
> I saw the sun rise.
> Then heard the cockerel crow.
> The tears burnt my eyes.
>
> Once more I discipline my flesh,
> again commit my inner self.
> In vain I tried to merge with earth.
> I need to face my task afresh.

[52] *Ruf* (1916), p. 18, first verse omitted.
[53] Ibid., p. 128.

Not for me the sanguine dream
of clever husband, life of normal bride.
A dark cross weighs my shoulders down.
My way grows straiter stride by stride.[54]

Many of these images refer to experiences of the immediate past such as estrangement from her first husband, the unsuccessful attempt to use the earth for stability and solace. Yet the premonitions of sacrificial suffering were to remain with her in the emigration. In 1938 she foresaw 'my end, my fiery end'[55]: the image finds its explanation in another poem of that year in which she finds herself brought to a pyre for her sins. It was written at a time when she was particularly burdened with accusations of transgressing the monastic Rule.

A judgment will take place before my death.
I shall be judged, and mercilessly judged.
They'll take away
my fine monastic garb,
the sisters will upbraid me,
enumerate my sins, appeal to law.
I shall be sentenced to be burned
and thus shall be professed once more.[56]

In concentrated form this unfinished poem conveys the essential thoughts of yet another poem of 1938.

The clerk will note the words,
with care the judges will apply the law.
They'll lead me off. Bells peal.
A trumpeter stands poised. I hear crowds roar.

Before me, a fiery and a glorious path.
The monks take care to keep the sacred flames alight.
The flickering embers of my life subside.
The end. (Why were the ropes so tight?)

---

[54] Ibid., p. 71, last verse omitted.
[55] *Stikhi* (1949), p. 59 (dated 17 April 1938).
[56] MS (30 December 1938), *MMP*; Hackel, *MM* (1980), p. 142. Draft of an unfinished poem.

Come, intersection of two beams,
come in the final throes.
For centuries, unseen, from wounds
that have not healed, blood flows.[57]

As it transpired, her execution in 1945 was to be devoid of
ceremonial. Yet fire was indeed to play its part in the procedure, for her body was ultimately to disappear into the
crematoria of Ravensbrück concentration camp.

After her death, her mother commented on her early poems:

From her youth she was convinced that suffering, trials,
agonizing death and incineration awaited her [. . .]. Liza
was young and full of life, and we did not believe in her
forebodings, whereas she believed in them firmly, though
she feared neither suffering nor death.[58]

---

[57] MS (17 April 1938), *MMP*; *Stikhi* (1949), 56–7. On the theme of the final
verse see Lev Gillet, 'Strazhdushchii Bog', *Pravoslavnoe Delo* (1939), pp. 9–
20, esp. p. 19.

[58] S. B. Pilenko, MS memoir, *MMP*; *Stikhi* (1949), p. 5.

8

WAR

Nor did she fear suffering and death when war brought Hitler's army into France during the catastrophic month of May-June 1940. On the contrary: 'I am not afraid to suffer,' she said to Mochul'skii, 'and I love death.'[1]

> Life's ledger is not going to be audited here, when it is as yet incomplete, but over there. And in the debit column will be listed two items only: a person's two births, or rather his two deaths; while in the credit column there will be the one word, 'eternity'.[2]

Comparable thoughts were contained in a poem which she had written on the occasion of Gaiana's death:

> No, death, it is not you that I have grown to love.
> Most vital in this life is that which is eternal.
> There is no deadlier process than to live.[3]

'If the Germans take Paris I shall stay here with my old women', she said on 21 May 1940, when the fall of Arras and Amiens was announced. 'Where else could I send them?' Some friends had urged her to leave Paris. 'But why should I leave? What threatens me here? Well, if the worst comes to the worst the Germans would shut me in a concentration camp. Yet people live on even in the camps.'[4] If some kind of move were to be contemplated, Russia alone held an attraction for her. 'I would prefer to perish in Russia rather

[1] *Mochul'skii*, p. 74.
[2] *MM* (1947), p. 132.
[3] MS (dated 2 June 1936), *MMP*; cf. *MM* (1947), p. 15.
[4] *Mochul'skii*, p. 74.

than starve to death in Paris.'[5] She was to cherish the prospect of such a return to the end. 'After the war I shall go to Russia', she said to a fellow prisoner in Ravensbrück. 'There will be a need to work there as in early Christian times, to propagate God's name by service, by means of one's whole life': 'to merge with one's native Church on native soil.'[6]

For some time before the war she had been aware of imminent disaster. In an article of November 1938 she wrote of the Nazi threat:

> Christianity at this time cannot close its eyes to the new and growing danger which surrounds the Church. Nor does it do so [. . .]. Yet however great this danger, whatever the disasters, upheavals, wars and persecutions with which the new paganism threatens us, at least something can be gained from all this; everything is clearly in its place, everyone must make their choice, there is nothing veiled or hypocritical in the enemy's approach.[7]

In a discussion group which met at I. I. Fondaminskii's flat she reiterated that she could sense the approach of an unprecedented catastrophe and added, 'Culture has come to a halt. We are entering eschatological times [. . .]. Do you not feel that the end is already near, that it is "at hand"?'[8] In the spirit of Revelation she concluded, 'Our aim is to hasten the end.'[9] Her characteristic concern for the ultimate limits of creation seemed to receive a new justification from the political and military developments of the day.

Nevertheless the initial success of the German war effort did not cause her to despair of an ultimate victory for the Allied cause. On 20 September 1940, at the height of the Battle of Britain, she asked Mochul'skii to make a note of her prediction: 'These are equinoctial gales. England is saved.

[5] Ibid.
[6] S. V. Nosovich, letter to F. T. Pianov (1955), *MMP*; S. V. Nosovich in *VRDP*, No. 2, p. 47.
[7] 'Rasizm i religiia', *Russkie zapiski* (1938), No. 11, p. 157 (a comment on the papal encyclical of 1937, *Mit brennender Sorge*).
[8] *Mochul'skii*, p. 72. Cf. 1 Peter 4:7.
[9] *Mochul'skii*, p. 72. Cf. Revelation 22:20.

Germany has lost the war.'[10] Likewise, when the USSR was invaded on 22 June 1941, she said, 'I have no fears for Russia. I know she will win. The day will come when we shall hear on the radio that the Soviet air force has destroyed Berlin. Then there will be a "Russian period" of history. Russia will stretch from the Arctic to the Indian Ocean. A great future awaits Russia. But what an ocean of blood.'[11]

Even in the darkest days of the war, in December 1941, in a poem based on a text of Isaiah (Isaiah 21:11–12 is paraphrased and in the process russified), she was to write:

At night a starless sky.
A distant dog, a bark.
Now the watchman sounds his warning.
Time for thieves to be about.

'Watchman, is it long till dawn?'
His voice comes from the dark:
'It's still night, but nearly morning.
Morning's coming, never doubt.'[12]

On 10 October 1939 a new priest arrived at Lourmel to replace Fr Kiprian Kern. Fr Dimitrii Klepinin (1904–44) – 'My spiritual son and former student, whom I love', as Bulgakov wrote to Sophia Pilenko that same week[13] – had been ordained as recently as 1937. He had served in the chapel of the Russian Student Christian Movement, then (from October 1938) also in the remote parish of Ozoir-la-Ferrière. He was Mother Maria's junior by a dozen years and utterly unlike her in temperament: a man of few words, calm and self-effacing. But regardless of age, temperament or experience, no more suitable appointment could have been imagined. With his unobtrusive dedication to the service of the underprivileged and needy, Orthodox Action entered a new

[10] *Mochul'skii*, p. 75.
[11] Ibid. Similar thoughts are to be found in an unpublished article of 1941, 'Razmyshleniia o sud'bakh Evropy i Azii', *MMP*.
[12] MS, *MMP*; Hackel, *MM* (1980), p. 151.
[13] Letter of 14 October 1939, *MMP*.

phase of its existence and Mother Maria, as never before, could be assured of constant spiritual support.

The Easter of 1940, the last before the Occupation, was celebrated at Lourmel with exceptional fervour. Despite war-time restrictions, an unusual number of people gathered at midnight for the solemn paschal procession around the building, symbolic of that first procession 'late on the sabbath day, as it began to dawn on the first day of the week', when the three women came to Christ's tomb, bearing spices, and as yet unaware of their irrelevance. To accommodate more people, the first part of the service – mattins – was held in the refectory of the house itself, where an altar table was set up for the occasion. Those who remained for the nocturnal Eucharist then crossed the dark courtyard to the church.

Mochul'skii noted how one verse of the gospel reading seemed to summarize for the participants the situation in what was soon to be a Nazi-dominated Europe: 'The light shineth in darkness; and the darkness overcame it not.'[14] 'Beyond the frail walls of the modest garage-church, the darkness of war, the darkness of the terrible spring of 1940': inside, by contrast, the radiance of the resurrection, the triumph over death. A host of candles cast their festive light on apple blossom, white lilac, lilies and narcissi. Fr Dimitrii, in a new set of white silk vestments (sewn and embroidered by Mother Maria for the occasion) repeatedly caused the candles to sway and flicker as he addressed their bearers with the triumphant exclamation, 'Christ is risen!' and evoked the traditional response, 'Risen indeed!' A joyful Mother Maria could be seen near the altar with tears in her eyes and her face lit from below by the candle in her hand.

Of Easter in wartime she wrote:

Now, at this very minute, I know that hundreds of people have encountered [. . .] death, I know that thousands upon thousands wait their turn. I know that mothers wait for the postman and tremble when a letter is delayed by more than

---

[14] John 1:6, RV margin.

101

a day. I know that wives and children in their peaceful homes feel the war breathing down their necks.

And finally I know, and I know it with all my being, with all my faith, with all the spiritual force with which a human being is endowed, that at this very moment God is visiting his world. And the world can accept this visitation, it can open its heart [. . .], and then our temporal, fallen life will be immediately assimilated to the depths of eternity, then our human cross will take on the features of the cross which is both human and divine, and in the very midst of our mortal sorrow we shall see the white robes of the angel who will proclaim to us, 'He who died is no longer in the tomb'. Then will mankind enter into the paschal joy of the resurrection.

Alternatively: perhaps things will be no worse than before, only the same. Yet once again, and not for the first time, men will have fallen and failed to accept or discover any way towards transfiguration [. . .] .

Lifeless mankind may continue to be gladdened by minor achievements and disappointed by minor failures. It may reject its vocation. Scrupulously and conscientiously it may drag the lid of its coffin up over its own head.[15]

Lest Russian émigrés serving in the French armed forces lose sight of ways towards transfiguration, she addressed them in 'A Letter to Soldiers': 'Take care of the innermost self, which is subject to far greater dangers than the outer man. Preserve yourself, preserve the purity of your youth, do not treat war as something natural, do not mistake the sin and horror of life for life itself.'[16]

The fall of Paris (14 June) and of France (21 June) served to highlight the dangers of which she spoke. Hunger and homelessness were aggravated by a disastrous slump in morale. However, it would be a luxury to indulge in ideological recriminations, noted Mother Maria: 'There will be hunger

[15] *MM* (1947), pp. 147–8.
[16] Pravoslavnoe Delo, 'Pis'mo k soldatam: pis'mo pervoe', *MMP*. Duplicated, and intended as the first of a series of such letters.

this winter. We must save those who might [otherwise] perish.'[17]

Towards the end of the summer the authorities of the fifteenth *arrondissement* declared the canteen at Lourmel to be a municipal one, and an imposing notice – CANTINE MUNICIPALE NO. 9 – was attached to the façade of the house. In the courtyard between the house and the church Mother Maria set up a stall for the sale of staple foods. Everything was obtained as cheaply as possible at Les Halles and sold at cost price.

The daily routine at Lourmel did not differ significantly from the pre-war pattern. There was the regular celebration of services, with the Liturgy on Wednesdays, Saturdays and Sundays at least. There was the daily preparation of the midday meal. As before, there was the preliminary visit to Les Halles: the resulting purchases could now serve as enrichment for the watery soups and stews which were delivered at noon from the *mairie* in rue Péclet. The afternoon was set aside for form-filling and accounts, which were Pianov's concern. Meanwhile Mother Maria would visit the sick or herself receive visitors. Lectures or discussions might still fill the evenings; and these, together with late visits or visitors, would bring a late end to the day.

The pre-war pattern: but how different the setting! Try as they might, there was less food available, and yet more people in need of it. Furthermore the personal problems brought to Mother Maria were inevitably exacerbated by the conditions of the Occupation. For 'the great city became a prison', as she wrote in June 1942. 'There is dry clatter of iron, steel and brass. Order is all.'[18]

For Russians in the Occupied Zone, the invasion of the USSR on 22 June 1941 brought new limitations. In Paris alone approximately one thousand émigrés were arrested. Among the arrested were close friends of Mother Maria's such as I. I. Fondaminskii and F. T. Pianov. All were sent to

[17] *Mochul'skii*, p. 75.
[18] From the poem 'Dukhov den' ', MS (dated 20 June 1942), *MMP*; *MM* (1947), pp. 24–30.

a detention camp at Compiègne, a hundred kilometres to the north-east of Paris. Other members of Orthodox Action were to become familiar with the camp before long.

One of those arrested on 22 June was I. A. Krivoshein. He was to be released within a month, and he returned to Paris with the intention of organizing aid not only for the prisoners of Compiègne, but also for their dependants. He turned for advice to S. F. Stern ('a man of exceptional kindness and subtlety'),[19] who had already busied himself over many years with the collection and distribution of funds for émigrés in need. It was Stern who advised him to approach Mother Maria. As a result a committee was covertly established at Lourmel, which (apart from Stern, Krivoshein and Mother Maria) included Fr Dimitrii Klepinin, R. S. Kliachkina and S. V. Medvedeva. The committee organized the preparation and dispatch of food parcels: the French Red Cross placed a lorry at its disposal once a week for the journey to Compiègne. The committee also raised and distributed funds to support the prisoners' families. Sergei Stern subsequently extended this work to benefit other victims of Nazi repression.[20]

Meanwhile there was a new development at Compiègne. From August 1941 prisoners were selected at random as hostages. Many were subsequently executed.[21] It was against this background that Fondaminskii came firmly to the decision that he should be baptized.

Ilia Isidorovich Fondaminskii (1880–1942) was a Jew, though in his beliefs he was far removed from the Orthodox Judaism of his wealthy parents. It was socialism which first commanded his loyalty at the turn of the century, and his

[19] Letter of I. A. Krivoshein to the author (1976).
[20] S. F. Stern was to avoid arrest. However, on the eve of the liberation of Paris (1944) he was to receive a visit from a member of the SS. The latter considered that he had not been treated with sufficient respect, knocked Stern to the ground and beat him about the head with his boots. Stern died in 1946 from a cancer of the face which could be traced back to this assault.
[21] By the end of the Occupation 29,660 hostages had been executed in France on the principle of collective responsibility for acts of sabotage and resistance.

revolutionary (at times, terrorist) activities had brought him into exile from Russia to France for the decade before 1917. He was to return to Russia after the February Revolution, there to take part in the Kerenskii administration and to be elected to the S-R Party's Central Committee. But the October Revolution left him with no part to play in the new establishment. Once more in exile, he returned to the same flat in Paris to which the *ancien régime* had once caused him to retire. Here, as never before, he was to add Christians, and particularly Christian socialists, to his wide range of friends and collaborators.

Fondaminskii, with his unfailing generosity, his self-abnegation and his child-like yet sober concern for the deprived or distressed, was to find a natural home in Orthodox Action. 'It is difficult to say who had the greater influence on whom, Mother Maria on him, or he on Mother Maria', remarked Pianov. 'But one thing may be asserted with confidence: they shared the same thoughts, the same language, the same ideal of Christian love [. . .]. At that time he was an unbaptized Jew. [Yet] he experienced in the Church something to which we, the conventional Orthodox, were deaf.'[22] His regular attendance at the services of Fr Lev Gillet's French-language parish certainly spoke of his commitment. But when people wondered why he remained unbaptized he would refer to his own unworthiness. Less often he would mention an additional reason for his delay, loyalty to his wife. She had died in 1935, without abandoning her attachment to the Jewish religious community despite her acceptance of the Christian faith, and he had earlier intended to remain at one with her in this respect. It was a consideration which also may have had a wider application: 'although he was not particularly concerned with Jewish problems, he had no wish to break his links with the Jewish people, above all his circle of friends and relatives, for whom the religious and the ethnic were inextricably linked.'[23] But whatever the reasons for his pro-

[22] F. T. Pianov, Memoir (1962), *MMP*.
[23] G. P. Fedotov, 'I. I. Fondaminskii v emigratsii', *Novyi Zhurnal*, No. 18 (1948), pp. 321–2.

longed catechumenate the time had now come to set them aside.

The camp at Compiègne had its makeshift Orthodox chapel, which had been set up in one of the barracks by a prisoner, Fr Konstantin Zambrzhitskii. A vigil was celebrated there on 20 September 1941 (it was the eve of one of the major feasts, the Nativity of the Mother of God), and this was followed by Fondaminskii's baptism and chrismation. At Fondaminskii's request, it was a private event: the baptism of a Jew was not expected to find favour with the Nazi authorities. Nevertheless the word may have spread. One way or another, the chapel was abruptly dismantled on the following day, and the Liturgy at which the newly baptized Ilia received his first communion had to be held in Fr Konstantin's cell. Pianov was the godfather: he recalled that Fondaminskii 'radiated a calm joy'.[24] 'I feel really well,' wrote Fondaminskii to his sister at about this time, 'it is a long time since I felt so calm, so cheerful, even happy.'[25] To a Parisian friend he wrote that he was now ready for anything, 'whether for life or death'. As never before 'he knew the nature of grace and had no need to search for words to express it.'[26]

Soon afterwards a gastric ulcer brought Fondaminskii to the local municipal hospital. Mother Maria was able to visit him there. A plan was devised for his flight via the Free Zone to the USA. It received the tacit approval of the hospital staff. But Fondaminskii rejected it firmly. He preferred undemonstratively to share the fate of his 'kinsmen according to the flesh'.[27] As G. P. Fedotov noted, 'In his last days he wished to live with the Christians and to die with the Jews.'[28]

He was not to be deflected from this resolve. In August 1942, on the very eve of his deportation from Drancy to the East, he appears to have rejected a second plan for his escape, in the preparation of which Mother Maria had once more

[24] F. T. Pianov, memoir (1962), *MMP*.
[25] Quoted by G. P. Fedotov, *Novyi Zhurnal*, No. 18 (1948), p. 327.
[26] S. M. Zernova, memoir (1962), *MMP*.
[27] Romans 9:3.
[28] G. P. Fedotov, *Novyi Zhurnal*, No. 18 (1948), p. 328.

played a leading role. Characteristically, in his last letter to her, he was concerned above all that his decision should cause his friends no pain: 'Let my friends have no worries about me. Tell them all that I am perfectly all right. I am completely happy. I never thought that there would be so much joy in God.' 'It is out of dough like this that saints are made', remarked Mother Maria.[29] The letter left her in tears.

All the arrangements had been made. That night he was to have been driven from Drancy to the comparative safety of the Parisian military hospital of Val-de-Grâce (Ve). Instead he was deported to Auschwitz, a willing victim, there to perish.[30]

The Russians who remained in Paris had now to register with an émigré 'leader', Iu. S. Zherebkov, a young Nazi recently arrived from Germany, who was placed at the head of a Directorate for Russian émigré affairs in France. This body issued apparently harmless identity cards to the Russians. But (in anticipation of a decree of 11 December 1942) it separately inscribed the cards of Russian Jews. It was already abundantly clear that this involved more than a technical distinction. To accept one type of card meant to facilitate the distribution of the other. Mother Maria and Fr Dimitrii were among those who scornfully ignored Zherebkov's demands. In so doing they risked arrest on the part of the German security police. Zherebkov had threatened that émigrés 'who are not registered in the required manner [. . .] will be treated as if they were citizens of the USSR', in other words enemy aliens.[31] For their part, the French police generally tended to overlook the breach of regulations like these.

Mother Maria had no time for the Zherebkovites, nor for

---

[29] Quoted by N. A. Teffi, 'Ilia Fondaminskii', *Russkoe Novoe Slovo*, 29 April 1953, p. 3.

[30] As far as is known, Fondaminskii died on 19 November 1942. Beginning on 10 August 1942 there were to be deportations from Drancy to the East on every other day that month. By the end of the year 31,983 Jews had been deported by this route. On Drancy see J. Darville and S. Wichené, *Drancy la juive ou la deuxième inquisition* (Cahan, Seine, 1945).

[31] *Parizhskii Vestnik*, No. 53 (19 June 1943), p. 3. This newspaper was published weekly (1942–3) by the Zherebkov Directorate, which was located at 4 rue de Galliéra, Paris XVIe.

their patrons. She believed Hitler's Germany to be the contaminator 'of all European springs and wells'. At the head of its master race, she wrote in 1941, 'stands a madman, a paranoiac, who ought to be confined to a madhouse, who needs a straitjacket and a cork-lined room so that his bestial wailing would not disturb the world at large.'[32] It was not easy, nor indeed was it wise, to write so explicitly with the Gestapo likely to call at the slightest provocation.

But Mother Maria had no desire to accommodate herself to the Occupation. When officials came to Lourmel to put up posters urging Frenchmen to work as volunteers in German factories, Pianov (who had been released from Compiègne in December 1941) would attempt to dissuade them. Mother Maria would simply tear the posters down from the walls. When it transpired that some of the tenants at the hostel in rue François Gérard were acting as pro-German collaborators, she preferred to let Orthodox Action yield control of the house to them. Although a considerable sum had been spent on the premises by the association, its committee simply refused to renew the lease.

Her forthrightness reflected her integrity: it also demonstrated a dangerous lack of discretion. She had no hesitation in challenging representatives of the new establishment on their basic presuppositions. More than once she received visits from a German pastor by the name of Peters. He claimed to be interested in her social work and discussed the ideals of Orthodox Action with her at some length. It was eventually established that he belonged to the Nazi-sponsored (and at one time powerful) *Deutsche Christen*, who sought to purge the Gospels of all non-aryan traces. 'But how could you possibly be both Christian and Nazi?' was her unequivocal response when he asserted that Christ was no Jew.[33] She was no less

[32] 'Razmyshleniia o sud'bakh Evropy i Azii' (1941), *MMP*.

[33] Mother Elizaveta [S. V.] Medvedeva, *o.* (1964). On the *Deutsche Christen* see J. S. Conway, *The Nazi Persecution of the Churches 1933–45* (London 1968), esp. p. 263. In the background of the denial that Jesus was a Jew were the writings of Houston Stewart Chamberlain (1855–1927), in particular his *Die Grundlagen des Neunzehnten Jahrhunderts* (Munich 1919), i. 246ff.

direct with visitors who claimed to come from the prefecture and yet to be Resistance personnel. 'I treated them with suspicion', noted Pianov drily. 'K. V. Mochul'skii agreed with me in this.'[34] They were the more suspicious of the pastor. For her part Mother Maria regretted and at times resented her colleagues' caution. In Pianov's words, 'she became increasingly sombre and on one occasion at Noisy-le-Grand we had an unpleasant confrontation which lasted the whole night through.'[35]

Once more she felt misunderstood and abandoned. As often before, she tested herself in verse. She recognized that her stance was proving tiresome and demanding both for herself and others. But was it mere wilfulness that prompted her decisions? Was not her situation willed by God? A poem of March 1942 concluded that her many years of work were necessarily to lead her downwards 'into loneliness, into the dark'.[36]

But the events of the following summer were to dispel her gloom and to end her sense of isolation. By autumn a new acquaintance could speak of her as 'joyful, like someone who has discovered the true way towards their particular heroic feat'.[37]

Not that the events were anything but tragic. The edicts of Zherebkov had already hinted at their nature. A major campaign against the Jews was being carefully prepared.

In other parts of occupied Europe such as Poland or the USSR the Nazi authorities had shown no inhibitions in the pursuit of what they were soon to designate as 'the Final Solution of the Jewish Problem'.[38] But in a country like France the Nazis preferred not to antagonize public opinion. The

---

[34] F. T. Pianov. MS memoir (1968), *MMP*.

[35] Ibid.

[36] MS (dated 19 March 1942), *MMP*; Hackel, *MM* (1980), p. 160.

[37] A. A. Ugrimov, memoir, *MMP*.

[38] The term could already be taken for granted at the notorious Wansee Conference of 20 January 1942 (Hans Buccheim *et al.*, *Anatomie des SS-Staates* [Olten and Freiburg im Breisgau 1965], ii. 393). But it had been used at least as early as September 1939 (Germaine Tillion, *Ravensbrück* [New York 1975], p. 171n).

deportation of several thousand German Jews to Vichy France (October 1940) or the deportation of another several thousand refugee Jews back to Germany from Occupied France (November 1940) was not expected to create undue anxiety for French Jewry. Nevertheless legislative and administrative measures were gradually being taken in respect of the latter which were to involve ever-increasing restrictions.

At the very least Jews were required to register. This required a definition of the term 'Jew'. The first French decree on the subject, an adaptation of the Nuremberg Laws (1935), was issued on 27 September 1940. *Inter alia* it stated that

> Recognized as Jews are those who belong or have belonged to the Jewish religion or who possess more than two Jewish grandparents [. . .]. Those grandparents are considered Jewish who belong or have belonged to the Jewish religion.

In other words, religious affiliations were to be taken into account as well as 'racial origins'. The definition was to be revised in April 1941, but the question of religion still played a significant part in the new text, which concluded:

> In case of doubt all persons are considered Jewish who belong or have belonged to the Jewish religious community.[39]

In the eastern territories no allowance was to be made for any case of doubt. On the contrary: in July 1942 Himmler was to write with some exasperation to one of his subordinates:

> I must ask you urgently to see that no formal definition of the term 'Jew' is published. We are simply tying our hands by dogmatizing in this stupid way. The occupied eastern territories will be cleared of Jews. The Führer has placed this difficult task on my shoulders. No one can relieve me

[39] Quoted in J. Lubetzki, *La Condition des Juifs en France sous l'Occupation allemande* (Paris 1945), p. 30.

of the responsibility. Nor can I allow anyone to enter into any discussion of my statement.[40]

But in France the legislation was taken to have some status and it was discussed. Moreover sufficient loopholes were perceived in it to justify numerous appeals by citizens who claimed that they had been wrongly classified as Jews. The ability to produce a baptismal certificate or the equivalent could act as a powerful argument in support of such a claim.

There was thus a new and urgent need for these certificates which might protect their possessors from degradation, isolation and ultimately (as could not yet be foreseen) deportation. Christians of Jewish origin tended to possess the required document. To Fr Dimitrii Klepinin at Lourmel came repeated requests to provide certificates for non-Christian Jews.

The reticent and deceptively mild Fr Dimitrii decided to risk his own freedom rather than that of his petitioners. In the event it meant risking his life. He decided that the most appropriate certification, which could withstand cross-checking in the diocesan records, would simply indicate membership of the Lourmel congregation. It was his conviction that Christ would also have perjured himself if confronted by the same need.[41] Mother Maria immediately and enthusiastically accepted his decision. Fr Dimitrii's card index was soon to contain the names of something like eighty new 'parishioners'.[42]

When some attempt to check on his activities was indeed made by a member of the diocesan administration, it was met with a firm response. While casting doubts on his correspon-

---

[40] Nuremberg Document No. 626, quoted in Hans Buccheim et al., Anatomie des SS-Staates (Olten and Freiburg im Breisgau 1965), ii. 374.

[41] Mother Elizaveta [S. V.] Medvedeva, o. (1964).

[42] T. F. Klepinina, letter to the author (1981). According to one Jewish source, 'hundreds' were to receive certificates of membership or else baptismal certificates proper (I. Shmulevich in Forward, 17 April 1948). On the subject of such 'mercy baptisms' see J. M. Snoek, The Grey Book (Assen 1969), pp. 26–9. Snoek lists comparable actions by a variety of Christian leaders in various parts of Europe. To his list might be added the name of another Russian émigré priest in the same fifteenth arrondissement of Paris, Fr Afanasii Nechaev (5 rue Pétel).

dent's motives, Fr Dimitrii also argued for the confidentiality of the records:

> In answer to your request that I submit a list of those newly baptized since 1940 I take the liberty of stating that all those who, regardless of external circumstances, have received baptism at my hands are by the same token my spiritual children and under my immediate care. Your request could only have been provoked by external pressures and dictated to you by considerations of public order. In view of this I am obliged to withhold the information requested.[43]

On 4 March 1942 a decision was taken in Eichmann's Berlin office: the yellow star of David (*Zionsstern* in Nazi terminology), a version of which was already a required sign of identification for the Jews of Germany, Poland and Czechoslovakia, should now be worn by the Jews of other occupied territories, including France. After some months of discussion and delay, the necessary decree was published in Occupied France. It was to be enforced from 7 June 1942. Each Jew over the age of six was required to wear the Star. Each was to be issued with three copies. To add further to the wearer's discomfiture he was required to surrender one clothing coupon in exchange.

At the outset the sinister implications and potential of the Star decree were not appreciated either by the Jews or their compatriots. In Paris, as throughout the country, there were protests and demonstrations. Non-Jews undertook to wear the Star or else parodies of it. Jews and non-Jews alike wore the Star with pride, a fact which perplexed and annoyed the Nazi authorities.[44]

---

[43] Quoted by G. A. Raevskii in *Russkaia Mysl'*, 1 August 1961. The enquiry evidently referred back to 1940 since any Jewish person, even with no more than two Jewish grandparents, who joined a Christian Church after 25 June 1940 was still considered Jewish according to one interpretation of the law (S. Lubetzki, *La condition des Juifs en France sous l'Occupation allemande* [Paris 1945], p. 30).

[44] L. Poliakov, *L'Etoile Jaune* (Paris 1949), pp. 43, 46–9, 78–92.

Monasticism 'in the world'.
Mother Maria in the yard
t Lourmel (1937).

9 *Monasticism 'in the world'*. Mother
Maria with Mother Evdokia (right)
and Mother Liubov' (left) outside
the house at Noisy (mid-1930s).

10 *Lay support*. Fedor Timofeevich
Pianov (late 1930s).

11 *Poetry*. The first draft of a poem by Mother Mari is followed by a fair copy. A cigarette burn mark the manuscript (*c.* 1933 (*MMP*).

12 *Isolation*. 'How burdensome each step becomes. Steeper and lonelier the way.' A self-portrait of *c.* 1937 in the margin of *Stikhi* (1937), p. 16 (*MMP*).

13 *Parish life*. A new priest arrives at Lourmel, autumn 1939. Left to right: Sophia Pilenko, Iura Skobtsov, Aleksei Babadjan, Mother Maria, Georgii Fedotov, Fr Dimitrii Klepinin and Konstantin Mochul'skii.

14 *Parish priest*. Fr Dimitrii Klepinin (autumn 1939).

15 *Embroidery*. Mother Maria at her work. A portrait by N. Verevkina (early 1940s).

16 *Supreme sacrifice*. Central figures the Last Supper embroidery which Mother Maria worked f the icon screen at Lourmel (1940–1).

17 *Victory over evil*. An embroidery worked by Mother Maria at Ravensbrück concentration camp in the style of the Bayeux tapestry to mark the Allied invasion of Normandy (summer 1944). The inscription (in an approximation to Anglo-Saxon) reads (left) *Then they came the Norsemen—the lofty fortress they besieged and within their arms befell the rich booty—*(right) *Fiercely they fought the brave invaders for the filthy devils were doomed to death—meanwhile rejoiced the peaceful folk.*

Mother Maria's immediate reaction to the decree was recorded in the poem which she wrote on the day of its promulgation. Unlike the main body of her verse, this was a public poem, or was destined to become one. Its circulation in Paris (it was well received in Jewish circles) once more served to draw attention to her independent stance.

Two triangles, King David's star.
No insult, this ancestral blazon.
It indicates a noble way.
It marks a chosen nation.

The final verse (the fifth) echoed and developed this introductory affirmation:

May you, stamped by this seal,
this star of David, by decree,
in your constrained response reveal
that you are spiritually free.[45]

She saw the persecution of the Jews as a challenge to all that Christendom held dear. As Pius XI had put it when he insisted that 'Antisemitism is unacceptable': 'Spiritually we are all Semites'.[46] 'There is no such thing as a Christian problem', said Mother Maria to Mochul'skii. 'Don't you realize that the battle is being waged against Christianity? If we were true Christians we would all wear the Star. The age of confessors has arrived. The majority will fall to temptation. But the Saviour said, "Fear not, little flock".'[47] In this battle, 'the persecuted Church, liberated from its union with the state, sees by its side its once vanquished sister, the Church of the Old Testament, likewise persecuted [. . .]. Between

<hr>

[45] MS (dated 7 June 1942), *MMP*; full text in Hackel, *MM* (1980), p. 163. Abbreviated text (with misreadings) in *Stikhi* (1949), p. 62.

[46] Pius XI, discourse to the directors of the Belgian Catholic Radio Agency (September 1938), quoted by Jacques Maritain, *Antisemitism* (London 1939), p. 27. Maritain (whom Mother Maria knew as one of Berdiaev's close friends) noted that 'no stronger word has been spoken by a Christian against antisemitism'.

[47] *Mochul'skii*, p. 75.

113

them, by the will of the outside world, is established a new and mysterious link.'[48]

It soon became evident that the Star decree was no more than a prelude. By a further decree of 8/15 July 1942 practically all public places were declared out of bounds to wearers of the Star, and all shopping was restricted to one hour per day, initially between three and four in the afternoon.[49] Many Jews began to detach the Star on leaving their homes or else avoided wearing it altogether. 'It seems to be equally dangerous whether you wear a Star or not', remarked Mother Maria.[50]

The dangers facing those who were liable to wear it were made devastatingly clear on the night of 15/16 July. That night mass arrests of Jews took place. A delay in putting the Occupation authorities' plan into operation allowed many potential victims to be forewarned. Even so, no less than 12,884 Jews were arrested, of whom 6,900 (including 4,051 children) were herded into the sports stadium – Vélodrome d'Hiver – on the Boulevard de Grenelle, a mere kilometre from Lourmel. In the course of five nightmarish days, the inmates could obtain water only from a single hydrant: ten latrines were supposed to serve them all. Many parents found themselves incapable even of looking after their own children. At the end of the five days, children were to be separated from parents, and for ever. They were sent via Drancy to Auschwitz. As Gerald Reitlinger has noted, 'Among all the unspeakable things of the Second World War, the story of the 4,051 children of the Vélodrome d'Hiver takes a very high place.'[51] Thus began the implementation of Himmler's secret order of 23 June 1942 to the effect that all the Jews of

---

[48] 'Razmyshleniia o sud'bakh Evropy i Azii' (1941), *MMP*. Meanwhile in Britain Fr Lev Gillet was about to publish an erudite and wide-ranging study on the perennial links between Christianity and Judaism: Lev Gillet, *Communion in the Messiah* (London 1942).

[49] Decree quoted in L. Poliakov, *L'Etoile Jaune* (Paris 1949), pp. 50–2.

[50] Mother Elizaveta [S. V.] Medvedeva, *o.* (1964).

[51] G. Reitlinger, *The Final Solution* (London 1953), p. 318.

France should be deported as soon as possible.[52]

Thanks to her monastic garb Mother Maria was able to gain admission to the stadium. She spent three days at work in the chaos. As best she could she comforted children, consoled their elders and distributed the woefully inadequate fragments of food which she had been able to bring with her. It is said that she managed to recruit some dustmen (who had been charged with the task of clearing the stadium of rubbish) in order to smuggle four young children to freedom in their bins.[53] But for her, as for all the others, it was the first experience of concentration camp conditions and she could only note with anguish how dwarfed a samaritan was by such a setting.

Beginning with the days immediately preceding the arrests of 15/16 July there was a pressing and unprecedented need for hiding places and escape routes for Jews. Lourmel acquired a new role. 'Lourmel is overcrowded', wrote Mochul'-skii. 'There are people in the wing and in the shed, there are people sleeping on the refectory floor. A whole family is sheltering in Fr Dimitrii's room, another in Iura's. Both Jews and non-Jews.' 'We have an acute accommodation crisis on our hands', remarked Mother Maris. 'It is amazing that the Germans haven't pounced on us yet.'[54] 'If the Germans come looking for Jews,' she said once, 'I'll show them the icon of the Mother of God.' 'The Mother of God, that might be all right', commented Berdiaev. 'But live Jews would be more of a problem.'[55]

Lourmel and Noisy became two of the links in the complex

---

[52] Quoted in a memorandum signed by Dannecker and Eichmann (Nuremberg Document 1223), translated in H. Monneray, ed., *La Persecution des Juifs en France et dans les autres pays de l'Ouest* [. . .] (Paris 1947), pp. 129–30. On the events of 15/16 July see pp. 142–53, 191, 197; also C. Lévy and P. Tillard, *La Grande rafle du Vél d'Hiv (16 juillet 1942)* (Paris 1967).

[53] T. Stratton Smith, *The Rebel Nun* (London 1965), pp. 190–3.

[54] *Mochul'skii*, p. 76.

[55] S. P. Zhaba, *o.* (1962) with minor corrections (1978). A variant of the conclusion is 'But Ottsup would be more of a problem'. The poet G. A. Ottsup [=Raevskii] (1897–1963), a baptised Jew, was a resident at Lourmel.

system of refuges and escape routes which grew up throughout France. Even Mother Maria's closest collaborators, such as Pianov, were often left in ignorance of their guests' precise destinations (many of them Catholic monasteries and convents). In the words of I. A. Krivoshein, 'It was no longer merely a question of material assistance. It was necessary to provide Jews with [forged] documents, to help them escape to the Southern as yet Unoccupied Zone, to find them a refuge in remote regions of the land. Furthermore it was necessary to make arrangements for children whose parents had been seized on the streets or in the course of raids.' Not only Jews and not only émigrés found shelter at Lourmel. 'In the kitchen, there worked for some time, until his transfer to the *maquis*, one of the first escaped Soviet prisoners of war with whom we came into contact.' Nor was he to be the last at Lourmel.[56]

The kitchen in question was also supplied with the help of Resistance personnel. One of the regular residents at Lourmel (N. Verevkina) put Mother Maria into contact with A. A. Ugrimov and his Dourdan Group. Ugrimov worked in a flour mill: 'Thus I was able to supply Mother Maria with bread ration cards, flour, groats and other products, at times using the mill lorry for the purpose.' And ('although neither of us spoke unduly about our respective Resistance concerns') all this was done in the awareness that the supplies were intended for fugitives from Nazi oppression, with all that this implied in terms of risk.[57]

Such centres as Lourmel or Noisy and such links as those with Dourdan were typical, for 'by its very nature the Resistance operated by means of small, often anonymous groups, dedicated to obscure and humble tasks . . . meeting, hurriedly separating, in perpetual movement, an enormous chain com-

[56] I. A. Krivoshein, 'Tak nam velelo serdtse' in *Protiv obshchego vraga* [. . .], ed. I. V. Parot'kin (Moscow 1972), pp. 270–1; I. A. Krivoshein, 'Mat' Mariia (Skobtsova) [. . .], *Zhurnal Moskovskoi Patriarkhii* (1970), No. 5, p. 39.
[57] A. A. Ugrimov, memoir, *MMP*. On the Dourdan Group see I. A. Krivoshein in *Protiv Obshchego Vraga* [. . .] ed. I. V. Parot'kin (Moscow 1972), pp. 277–80.

posed of a multitude of links which – how often! – broke [. . .].
To the surface would rise faces whose real names one did not
know, then would disappear, leaving no trace.'[58] The links at
Lourmel and Noisy were to survive until February 1943.

On the morning of Monday 8 February Pianov was at
Noisy while Mother Maria was out of town for a visit to her
former husband's wartime home at Les Feuillardes. The refectory at Lourmel was beginning to fill with customers in
anticipation of the midday meal. Iura Skobtsov was passing
through it when he was suddenly seized and searched by two
uniformed officers of the Nazi security police. In his pocket
was found a letter from a Jewish woman (Gavronskaia) to
whom Iura used to bring encouragement and advice. It was
addressed to Fr Dimitrii and contained a belated request for
a baptismal certificate.[59] The letter was in Russian. But Hans
Hofmann, the plainclothes Gestapo officer who completed
and headed the group of investigators, was a Baltic German
with Russian as his second language, Hence, indeed, his as-
signment to Lourmel.[60] It was the sort of letter that he needed.
Iura was taken to the office of Orthodox Action.

Iura's grandmother made her way there as soon as she
learned of the arrest. But Hofmann met her with abuse. 'Get
yourself out of here!' he shouted. 'Where's your priest? Let's
have your priest here.' When Fr Dimitrii appeared Hofmann
declared that Iura was to be taken as a hostage. He would be
released as soon as Mother Maria and Pianov appeared.

'When Iura was taken away,' wrote Sophia Pilenko subsequently, 'I was allowed to approach him. We embraced
and I blessed him, never imagining that this was our final
parting [. . .]. He was everyone's favourite, kind, reserved,
humble and prepared to give anyone his help.'[61]

Iura Skobtsov's childhood had been lacking in comfort and

[58] I. Schneersohn in D. Knout, *La résistance juive en France 1940–1944* (Paris
1947), p. 7.
[59] The sender of the letter was subsequently arrested. She perished in
Auschwitz.
[60] A group photograph of the Paris Gestapo shows Hofmann: reproduced
in Jacques Delarue, *The History of the Gestapo* (London 1964), p. 369.
[61] S. B. Pilenko, MS memoir, *MMP*; *MM* (1947), p. 151.

domesticity. His mother lacked the time, his father the parental skills, to provide for him adequately. It was a disturbing background. However with adolescence he was able to develop a positive attitude to it. A healthy piety encouraged ever-increasing appreciation of his mother's work, the price of which he had helped to pay. A sober enthusiasm informed his studies in architecture and town planning at the Sorbonne. The friendship of an outstanding scholar, Konstantin Mochul'skii (who was to dedicate his celebrated study of Dostoevskii to him)[62], developed his confidence and widened his perspectives.

But to Hofmann he was nothing other than a useful hostage. He had the house searched, the identity papers of Fr Dimitrii and S. V. Medvedeva impounded, and Iura driven away. No sooner had the security police left the premises than messengers were sent to inform Mother Maria and Pianov of the day's ominous events.

Iura's arrest involved more than the simple deprivation of liberty. Hundreds of hostages had already been shot. In this awareness Mother Maria set off for Paris the next morning. She had refused Daniil Skobtsov's offer to go in her stead: he would simply be arrested as a second hostage and she would still be required to appear. It would be preferable to have him work for Iura's release. 'If need be, put all the blame on me', she said as they walked to the station. 'Don't spare me, but get him out. I am strong, I can bear it. In any case the war will end soon. The main thing is to have Iurochka released.'[63] Outwardly she was calm and confident.

Meanwhile Pianov was giving parting instructions at Noisy (where several fugitives were sheltering). He was also soon to make his way to Paris.

The papers of Fr Dimitrii and Sophia Medvedeva had been impounded as a surety against their appearance on the following day at Gestapo headquarters. Fr Dimitrii had been there before. When Mother Maria had once been summoned for an inconclusive confrontation with the same Hofmann in

[62] K. Mochul'skii, *Dostoevskii: zhizn' i tvorchestvo* (Paris 1947), p. 5.
[63] D. E. Skobtsov in *MM* (1947), p. 155 (cf. *Mochul'skii*, p. 76).

118

the summer of 1942 he had volunteered to accompany her. But no visit to the rue des Saussaies was lightly undertaken, and the one now in prospect was undoubtedly more fraught with danger than the last. Fr Dimitrii rose early on the ninth to celebrate what was to prove his last Eucharist as a free man.

During the Occupation Fr Dimitrii had set up a small side-chapel in a brick appendage to the Lourmel church.[64] It was dedicated to St Philip, martyred Metropolitan of Moscow (1507–69). The appropriateness of the dedication was now to be revealed: for St Philip was killed for daring to criticize the bestial actions of his ruler (Ivan IV) and thus 'laid down his life for his flock'.[65] It was here that the service took place that morning. Immediately afterwards the two suspects set out on the lengthy journey to the former Ministry of the Interior which the Nazi security police now had for their seat.

After all this time the security police did not appear to have prepared their case against Orthodox Action with any care. Even the previous day's search had not provided them with anything of substance. They had found plenty of New Testaments. But they had ignored evidence of Anglo-American aid (which had continued to penetrate to Lourmel until the previous November) and Sophia Medvedeva had later been able to destroy it. They also failed to find such articles as Mother Maria's 'Razmyshleniia o sud'bakh Evropy i Azii' (1941) in which the Nazi system was scornfully criticized and derided. At her interrogation on the ninth S. V. Medvedeva was faced with puerile accusations which she did not find it difficult to parry:

'You are communists.'
'But we have a church.'
'It is only a cover.'

---

[64] Icons painted and embroidered by Mother Maria for the chapel are reproduced in Hackel, *One, of Great Price* (1965), p. 3; and Hackel, *MM* (1980), pl. 8.
[65] Words of a prayer to St Philip, quoted at the conclusion of G. P. Fedotov's study of his life, *Sviatoi Filipp Mitropolit Moskovskii* (Paris 1928).

'You are in power at present: you can think and act as you please.'
'So you think we are not permanently in power?'
'That's as God wills.'[66]

After further interrogation she was released with a firm warning about her future behaviour. It was a warning which was to be repeated several times on subsequent occasions when the security police found her at Lourmel, still persisting with the household duties which had been forbidden her. However, no action was taken. It may be that a minor point in her favour was that she had earlier registered as required at the Zherebkov office. German respect for correct, if meaningless, bureaucratic procedure could bring unexpected benefits as here. Nevertheless she withdrew from the capital when the work at Lourmel was finally disrupted and sought shelter with Mother Evdokia at Moisenay-le-Grand.

Fr Dimitrii was interrogated for four hours. He made no attempt to exculpate himself. Later, at Lourmel, Hofmann was to describe how he was offered his freedom on the condition that he helped no more Jews. Fr Dimitrii had raised his pectoral cross, shown the figure on it and asked, 'But do you know *this* Jew?' He was answered with a blow to the face. 'Your priest did himself in', stated Hofmann. 'He insists that if he were to be freed he would act exactly as before.'[67]

When Mother Maria arrived in Paris that day she first made her way to friends in order to establish a clearer picture of the events at Lourmel. On the tenth of February she returned home. Hofmann duly appeared and began her interrogation. But Iura was not released. Nor was he released

---

[66] Mother Elizaveta [S. V.] Medvedeva, *o.* (1960).
[67] Ibid.; also G. A. Raevskii in *Russkaia Mysl'*, 1 August 1961. As if anticipating the incident with the crucifix, Mother Maria had written in 1941: 'The Son of David, the Messiah whom his people once failed to accept, is now crucified together with those who once offered him no recognition' ('Razmyshleniia o sud'bakh Evropy i Azii', *MMP*). The Confessing Church in Germany was moved to use similar terms in 1943: 'along with Israel it is the Church and her Master, Jesus Christ, who are being assaulted' (quoted by J. S. Conway, *The Nazi Persecution of the Churches 1933–45* [London 1968], p. 264).

when Pianov presented himself at the rue des Saussaies on the evening of 16 February. Nevertheless Pianov himself remained under arrest.

The SIPO-SD officer who accompanied Hofmann visited the kitchen where Anatolii Viskovskii was at work. Viskovskii appeared to be of little interest to him, and he was not even questioned. But he was not to be forgotten. A few days later Hofmann returned to the house and ordered his arrest. He also arrested Iu. P. Kazachkin, who chanced to be in the house on a visit to the Klepinin family. In view of these encroachments and Hofmann's barely veiled threats, Fr Dimitrii's wife Tamara Fedorovna was soon to leave Paris with her two young children, the one four years, the other barely six months old.

Hofmann's behaviour suggested that he was at least well informed about Lourmel's residents and visitors. Not long before the February events a woman had arrived at Lourmel for shelter. Only recently had she been released by the Germans from detention. Even from her own accounts of prison it was clear that she had received preferential treatment. It later transpired that she was on friendly terms with Hofmann. Sophia Pilenko warned Mother Maria to be cautious: this was a spy. Characteristically she answered, 'It is not right to suspect people.'

It was Hofmann himself who was to confirm that such suspicions were in order. After Mother Maria's arrest, he remarked to Sophia Pilenko, 'Our agent sat at table with you.' 'Those of us who were left tried to guess who this Judas might have been', commented Sophia Pilenko, being scrupulously fair. 'There were suspicious people, but one could be mistaken, and only God knows for certain.'[68]

In any case there is no reason to suppose that Lourmel was undermined as the result of any one informer's work. Enough of a reputation had been established and enough rumours were rife to make the arrests probable regardless of what agents might report. Many such rumours had their source in

[68] S. B Pilenko, MS memoir, *MMP*.

Mother Maria's readiness to accept people at their face value and to confide in them. Many owed their wide circulation to the zeal and venom of right wing circles in the Russian emigration.

Hofmann took his time with the interrogation. He then ordered Mother Maria to be searched. 'You brought your daughter up badly,' he shouted at the octogenarian Sophia Pilenko, 'all she can do is help yids!'[69] When Pianov was later taunted in a similar manner he replied, 'Help was given to anyone in need, Jew and non-Jew alike. It is the duty of any Christian to afford such help.'[70] Sophia Pilenko answered in similar terms:

> My daughter is a genuine Christian, and for her there is neither Greek nor Jew, only individuals in distress. If you were threatened by some disaster, she would help you too.

Mother Maria smiled at this and said, 'Yes, I suppose I would.'[71] The remark left Hofmann nonplussed.

But he had no further cause to linger. The security police car was ready in the street. In Sophia Pilenko's words:

> We embraced. I blessed her. We had lived all our life together, in friendship, hardly ever apart. She bade me farewell and said, as she always did at the most difficult moments of my life (such as when she told me of my son's death and later of my granddaughter's), 'Mother, be strong'.

Hofmann returned on the following day with the assurance, 'You will never see your daughter again'.[72]

---

[69] Ibid.; also *MM* (1947), p. 152.
[70] F. T. Pianov, *o.* (1964).
[71] S. B. Pilenko, MS memoir, *MMP*; also *MM* (1947), p. 152.
[72] Ibid.

9

MARTYRDOM

Orthodox Action was dissolved by order of the Occupation authorities. Its initiator found confinement in the fort at Romainville tedious but tolerable. 'We are all four of us together', wrote Mother Maria to Lourmel. 'I am in a large hall with thirty-four women. We have exercise twice a day. We rest, we have plenty of free time. You are worse off than we are.' But she added, 'I hope that this is not for long.'[1] The tension of the previous weeks was left behind. Pianov saw her in the exercise yard: 'Mother Maria was unrecognizable, cheerful and friendly.'[2]

They were soon to be separated. On 27 February Pianov was taken together with Iura and Fr Dimitrii back to the rue des Saussaies, this time en route for Compiègne.

> About four hundred of us were assembled in the yard [. . .].
> Fr Dimitrii, with his cassock torn, was made into a laughing stock. One of the SS began to prod and beat him, calling him *Jude*. Iura Skobtsov, who stood beside him, was in tears. Fr Dimitrii began to console him, saying that Christ withstood greater mockery than this.

While Fr Dimitrii could humbly tolerate personal attacks on himself, noted Pianov, 'the degradation of others caused him anguish, even physical pain'.[3]

On 21 April Daniil Skobtsov came to Romainville with a parcel for Mother Maria. He was not admitted. According to the guards she had already been transferred elsewhere. As he

---

[1] *Mochul'skii*, pp. 76–7. For reasons of censorship the postcard was written in French. The 'large hall' was known as cell No. 101.
[2] F. T. Pianov, MS memoir (1968), *MMP*.
[3] *VRDP*, No. 1, p. 8.

returned to the Metro a convoy of coaches had passed him on their way to the prison. An instinct prompted him to leave his train and to retrace his steps. Within fifteen minutes of his return the same coaches emerged from the fort, packed with women who cheered and sang. In the third coach he saw Mother Maria. 'Mother Maria also saw me, jumped up from her seat and waved energetically.'[4] She too was on her way to Compiègne, albeit for an unexpectedly short stay.

The camp at Compiègne was to be the scene of her last meeting with Iura. At the end of the day, when the visiting kitchen staff were allowed to leave the camp, Iura seized the opportunity to mingle with them and to cross the barrier which separated the male and female barracks. From dusk to dawn the two were together. As Iura was to explain to Pianov, 'each strengthened the other's resolve to bear everything without fear'. The sunrise of 22 April was to be remembered with particular poignancy by them both. It provided a reminder of the moment in the Orthodox All Night Vigil service, where the rising of the sun is accompanied by the exclamation 'Glory to thee, who hast shown us light'; it also pointed forward to the ultimate 'rising of the sun which has no setting',[5] the inauguration of the celestial city 'where there shall be no night'.[6] After they had parted, Mother Maria stood for some time gazing into the distance, quietly weeping.

'My most dear and precious ones', wrote Iura to Lourmel. '[. . .] You probably know already that I saw mama on the night of her departure for Germany, she was in a remarkable state of mind and told me [. . .] that I must trust in her ability to bear things and in general not to worry about her. Every day we remember her at the *proskomidia* (and you as well)':[7] 'We celebrate the Eucharist and receive communion each day.'[8]

'Our church is a very good one', wrote Fr Dimitrii: a

[4] *MM* (1947), p. 158.
[5] *Stikhi* (1937), p. 10.
[6] Revelation 22:5.
[7] Original in the papers of D. E. Skobtsov (1964); copy in *MMP*.
[8] *Mochul'skii*, p. 77.

barrack room had once more been transformed for the purpose, this time with the help of ordinary camp tables and beds (some of which stood on their side to make an icon screen and a reading stand). It was a gratifying victory of ingenuity and devotion over necessity, and Fr Dimitrii recorded it in a drawing for his wife.[9]

The prisoners at Compiègne were to be Fr Dimitrii's last parishioners and the memory of his ministry in this setting was to be treasured by Fedor Pianov to the end of his days. Soon after his eventual release from the camps in 1945 he was to write:

I was acquainted with Dima Klepinin (subsequently Fr Dimitrii) for twenty-three years but really came to know and understand him only a year before his death. We spent about a year together in the camp at Compiègne. Without exaggeration I can say that the year I spent with him was a godsend. I do not regret that year.

The basic, ultimate questions of life are decided by each person individually and God alone can assist in this. But from my experience with Fr Dimitrii I can confidently assert that God can also speak through another individual. From my experience with him I learned to understand what enormous spiritual, psychological and moral support one man can give to others as a friend, companion and confessor [. . .]. Now, in freedom, I often bitterly regret the gradual loss of that which God granted me to gain from Fr Dimitrii.[10]

Iura also found that his imprisonment was bringing him unexpected benefits.

Thanks to our daily Eucharists our life here is quite transfigured and to tell the honest truth I have nothing to complain of, the four of us live together in brotherly love, Dima and I speak to each other as *tu* and he is preparing me for

[9] In the papers of T. F. Klepinina; reproduced in T. Stratton Smith, *The Rebel Nun* (London 1965), p. 223.
[10] *VRDP*, No. 1, p. 7.

the priesthood. God's will needs to be understoood. After all, this attracted me all my life and in the end it was the only thing I was interested in, though my interest was stifled by Parisian life and the illusion that there might be 'something better' – as if there could be anything better.[11]

The group commanded Fr Dimitrii's loyalty to the same degree. When there seemed to be an opportunity to arrange his separate release through the intervention of Pastor Peters, he responded firmly, 'Do not intercede for me alone, my solidarity is with the whole group of Orthodox Action.'[12]

All were liable to be sent to Germany for forced labour. But Iura preferred this prospect to any collaborationist alternative. 'The other day they registered us all,' he wrote to his father and grandmother on 16 August 1943, 'there are suppositions that this is maybe done in order to enrol us in Vlasov's army, if so I prefer to remain in Compiègne or to be sent to Germany as a worker.'[13] Exactly four months later it was Germany that proved to be his destination.

On 16 December Iura and Fr Dimitrii were included in a detachment of Compiègne prisoners who were suddenly deported to Buchenwald concentration camp. Three weeks later Pianov caught up with them there. But they were soon to be parted again. Long before dawn on 25 January 1944 (it was about 4 a.m.) Pianov had a brief meeting with them just before they were due to be taken further.

It was a cold frosty morning [. . .], there was intense darkness and the camp was [thus] lit throughout by strong projectors. On the other side of the wire stood Fr Dimitrii and Iura in striped gowns, jackets and trousers, canvas boots with wooden soles and light berets on their closely

[11] Letter to his relatives, original in the papers of D. E. Skobtsov (1964); copy in *MMP*.
[12] T. F. Klepinina, personal communication (1978, 1981). Pastor Peters was working with the *Evangelisches Hilfwerk für Internierte und Kriegsgefangene*, which had an office at 25 rue Blanche, Paris IXe.
[13] MS, *MMP*. Vlasov's army was being recruited from Soviet prisoners and Russian émigrés to fight in Hitler's 'crusade against communism' on the eastern front.

cropped heads [. . .]. Fr Dimitrii had been shaved. They hastily announced that they were being sent as part of a transport to Dora, forty kilometres from Buchenwald. As we parted both asked me to bless them, which I did, and for my part asked them to bless me. They vanished into the cold darkness.[14]

Pianov was to remain in Buchenwald until April 1945.[15] He was liberated in the final stages of one of the death marches ordered by the Nazis in a vain attempt to clear the camps as the Allied armies approached them.[16] But his former companions were not to survive even into the last year of the war.

The camp at Dora was barely established and callously ill-organized. Prisoners were required to live and work underground, where tunnels were being excavated and factories built for the manufacture of parts for the V1 and V2 rockets. The camp's death rate was a by-word even in Buchenwald, whose crematoria disposed of Dora's dead during that first year of its existence.

Within ten days of his arrival, Iura Skobtsov (prisoner 38,893) was infected with furucolosis: his body was covered with boils. He was deposited in the camp *Revier*, the space designated as an infirmary, but as yet provided with no medical equipment whatsoever. On about 6 February, in his twenty-fourth year, he was despatched for what the authorities euphemistically termed treatment to 'an unknown destination'. Iurii Kazachkin, who had preceded the others to Dora, was able to embrace him as he was about to leave. Iura was calm.

[14] F. T. Pianov, MS memoir (1968), *MMP*; also *o.* (1960 and 1964).
[15] In August 1944 he was to encounter I. A. Krivoshein in the camp. By then he was an experienced prisoner, and he was able to offer Krivoshein invaluable advice and support. Igor' Krivoshein had been arrested in June 1944. In Paris he was tortured by the Gestapo and originally sentenced to death before being transported to Buchenwald via Compiègne. On Krivoshein's Resistance work see *VRDP*, No. 1, pp. 35–48 and *Protiv obshchego vraga* [. . .], ed. I. V. Parot'kin (Moscow 1972), pp. 274–7.
[16] Anatolii Viskovskii, who had arrived in Buchenwald together with Iura and Fr Dimitrii, was on the same march. He died within twenty-four hours of his liberation (23 April 1945).

Two days later in the same *Revier* Kazachkin found his old friend Fr Dimitrii, who had just been granted a *Schonung*: this freed him from the obligation to work on account of ill health. But the *Schonung* had come too late. Fr Dimitrii lay on the ground in the *Revier* (there was no floor): he was dying of pneumonia. Earlier he had spoken of extreme weakness and dejection, of feeling forsaken by God.[17] Now he lacked the strength to speak. That day prisoners had been issued a card on which to write home. Fr Dimitrii's card was to remain blank. But he died with this potential link with his wife and children in his hand. Early in the morning of 10 February his body was sent by lorry to Buchenwald for cremation.

A letter from Iura, written on the eve of the fatal departure for Germany, was the last to convey his friend's blessing and to reveal the spirit in which they both then faced their end.

> My dears, Dima [Fr Dimitrii] blesses you, my most beloved ones. I am to go to Germany with Dima, Fr Andrei[18] and Anatolii [Viskovskii]. I am absolutely calm, even somewhat proud to share mama's fate. I promise you I will bear everything with dignity. Whatever happens, sooner or later, we shall all be together. I can say in all honesty that I am not afraid of anything any more: my chief anxiety is you, I would be thoroughly content if I could leave in the awareness that you are calm and that you possess that peace of which no powers can ever deprive us. I ask anyone whom I have hurt in any way to forgive me. Christ be with you![19]

In the laconic words of the ten year old who was asked to describe the deportations, 'Ils allèrent à l'autre bout de la terre et ils ne sont pas revenus.'[20]

[17] Iu. P. Kazachkin, quoted by F. T. Pianov, memoir, *MMP*. Iurii Kazachkin was to be liberated in 1945, but he returned to Paris with his health broken. He died in 1968.

[18] Protopresbyter Andrei Vrasskii, who was also to perish in the camps (1944).

[19] Copy in the hand of S. B. Pilenko, *MMP*; *MM* (1947), p. 153. The letter was found in the suitcase of Iura's possessions which was returned to Paris from Compiègne.

[20] Inscription at the Memorial to the Deportation (Paris Ve).

On the morning which followed her meeting with Iura, Mother Maria was brought to Compiègne station together with over two hundred other women, who were to form transport No. 19,000, the first to take this particular route as deportees.[21] They were sealed into cattle trucks. Their traumatic journey eastwards, without water or any form of sanitation, was to last three days. Unknown to them, they passed through Berlin, crossed the desolate forests and marshes of Mecklenburg province and finally arrived at the obscure railway station of Fürstenberg. It was a station that was to achieve a new and dismal prominence as the result of its proximity to Ravensbrück concentration camp.

In this camp Mother Maria (prisoner 19,263) was to spend the last two years of her life. Never had she been faced with such extreme or widespread (nor such consciously contrived) misery. The Vélodrome d'Hiver as an exceptional experience was one thing: hitherto its extension, intensification and perpetuation as a norm would have seemed inconceivable.

Mother Maria possessed many characteristics which could facilitate survival. The fact that she knew the cause of her arrest made her confinement less unreasonable. Her personal faith made possible the justification and therefore the acceptance of suffering. The death of her two daughters (as well as several hundred funerals at Lourmel)[22] had familiarized her with death. In any case she looked to the resurrection of the dead and had no fear of death itself. At the same time she had a well-developed instinct for self-preservation as the result of her experiences since the Revolution of 1917. She was physically and morally strong, and – notwithstanding her naivety in certain respects – she was shrewd. Her sense of humour could provide a defence against the intolerable and the incomprehensible. Yet another defence was provided by

[21] Amicale de Ravensbrück [. . .], *Les françaises à Ravensbrück* (Paris 1965), p. 58; Rosane Lascroux, memoir, *MMP*.

[22] Free funerals were arranged at Lourmel for those who died destitute. At one stage Mother Maria remarked that the church was gradually turning into a cemetery chapel: 'there are funerals almost every day' (*Mochul'skii*, p. 70). Mother Maria kept a record of the departed by embroidering their names on a large cloth, which was displayed in the church.

the way of life on which she had embarked long before her imprisonment. This had accustomed her to a lack of privacy and personal security, the enforced and unprecedented loss of which disorientated and undermined so many of her fellow inmates. This same way of life had accustomed her to give rather than to garner. She was thus in a position to counteract that egotism which became a dominant force in the life of the average prisoner for whom 'behaviour was reduced to survival activities'.[23]

Mother Maria's convoy was initially sheltered from the full horror of the camp by two long months of quarantine, which confined the newly registered prisoners to a single block. But even full exposure to the camp was not to bring her to despair. On the contrary (as one of her fellow prisoners remembered):

> She was never downcast, never. She never complained [. . .]. She was full of good cheer, really good cheer. We had roll calls which lasted a great deal of time. We were woken at three in the morning and we had to stand out in the open in the middle of winter until all the barracks were counted. She took all this calmly and she would say, 'Well that's that, yet another day completed. And tomorrow it will be the same all over again. But one fine day the time will come for all of this to end.'[24]

The camps provoked selectivity in friendship: 'It was impossible to radiate friendship on good and bad alike; we had little enough in the camp which we could share. Each person had to select those to whom he would be prepared to give support.'[25] Inevitably, Mother Maria belonged to a particular group. Her background and her location in the camp determined that its members tended to be French or Russian or a mixture of the two. But she had no wish to limit her network of mutual aid to prisoners of any one nationality, party or religion. In the words of Solange Périchon,

[23] H. A. Bloch, 'The personality of inmates of concentration camps', *American Journal of Sociology*, vol. 52 (1946–7), p. 336.
[24] Solange Périchon, *o.* (1964).
[25] B. Kautsky, *Teufel und Verdammte* (Zurich 1946), p. 178.

She was on good terms with everyone [. . .]. Anyone in the block, no matter who it was, knew her on equal terms. She was the kind of person who made no distinction between people [. . .]. She got on well with the young and elderly, with those who held extremely progressive political views and those whose religious beliefs differed radically from hers. She allowed nothing of secondary importance to impede her contact with people.[26]

Thus (confirms Rosane Lascroux) 'She exercised an enormous influence on us all. No matter what our nationality, age, political convictions – this had no significance whatever [. . .]. Mother Maria was adored by all.'[27] The younger prisoners gained particularly from her concern: 'She took us under her wing [. . .]. We were cut off from our families, and somehow she provided us with a family.'[28]

The influence exerted by Mother Maria depended on her concern for the individual. But she also made a contribution to the community's welfare by playing a public role as speaker or discussion group leader. She had begun to play such a role already during the tense weeks of her company's quarantine. She gave numerous talks on Russian and Orthodox church history.[29] In the camp proper she was to continue the practice.

She used to organize real discussion circles, seated on her palliasse, and I had the good fortune to participate in them [wrote Jacqueline Péry]. Here was an oasis at the end of a terrible day. She would tell us of her social work, about how she conceived the reconciliation of the Orthodox and Catholic Churches. We would question her about the history of Russia, about its future, about communism, about her frequent contacts with the young women from the Soviet army, with whom she liked to surround herself. These discussions, whatever their subject matter, provided an escape from the hell in which we lived. They allowed us

[26] Solange Périchon, o. (1964).
[27] Rosane Lascroux, memoir (1975), *MMP*.
[28] Solange Périchon, o. (1964). She was twenty years old at the time.
[29] I. N. Webster, *MM* (1947), p. 161.

131

to restore our depleted morale, they rekindled in us the flame of thought, which barely flickered beneath the heavy burden of horror.

Towards the end of such sessions 'Mother Maria would take up a *Manuel du Chrétien* which one of the prisoners had managed to retain when she was searched, and would read a passage from the Gospels and Epistles. Together we would provide a commentary on the texts and then meditate on them. Often we would conclude with compline. In retrospect this period seemed like paradise to us.'[30] However, although 'she prayed with believers and read the Gospels [with them]', noted another prisoner, 'she never preached [to outsiders], but discussed religion [simply] with those who sought it, causing them to understand it and to exercise their minds, not merely their feelings. Wherever and however she could, she would sustain the as yet incompletely extinguished flame of humanity, no matter what form it took.'[31]

The camp system aimed at the extinction of this flame: it sought to exploit, degrade and brutalize the inmates before bringing about their untimely death. Mother Maria's will and capacity to withstand the brutalization was demonstrated in an incident which she described to Sophia Nosovich.

I was walking between the ranks before roll call so as to warm myself up a little. I started talking to one of the Russian girls and failed to notice an SS woman who interrupted me in mid-sentence by striking me painfully in the face with a leather strap. I finished the sentence which I had begun in Russian and without a glance at her. I had the feeling that she wasn't really present there before me.

In Nosovich's judgement, 'it was not submissiveness which gave her strength to bear the suffering, but the integrity and wealth of her inner life.'[32] Moreover she was convinced that evil was an ephemeral force. 'I often suspect that hell is here

[30] Jacqueline Péry, memoir, *MMP*.
[31] S. V. Nosovich, memoir, *MMP*.
[32] S. V. Nosovich, memoir, *MMP*; cf. her account in *VRDP*, No. 2, p. 48.

on earth', she would say in the camp. 'Beyond the confines of this life there is no such thing. Eternal evil cannot exist.'[33] In this she echoed the teachings of Berdiaev,[34] while differing from many a seasoned prisoner who had yet another reason for experiencing no positive hatred (as opposed to contempt) for the SS and their assistants. As is noted by two veterans of Auschwitz, their behaviour was too outrageous for them to become the object of hate, since hate implies a personal relationship: 'a man is hated for his "human" qualities, not his "inhuman" ones. The "beast" only inspires fear, abhorrence, or disgust.'[35]

It was not a question of repression: in Mother Maria's estimation, withdrawal from experience could threaten, while it seemed to safeguard, human dignity. Such withdrawal might begin with a salutary emergency repression of normal feelings on first encountering the camps. More sinister was the eventual acceptance of obscenity as a norm: after only a few weeks of camp life 'the suffering, illness, dying and death of human beings became such a common sight [. . .] that it no longer had the power to move.'[36] Sophia Nosovich complained to Mother Maria of the deadening effect of such acclimatization: 'I once said to her that it was more than a question of my ceasing to feel anything whatsoever, my very thought process was numbed and had ground to a halt.' 'No, no,' responded Mother Maria, 'whatever you do, continue to think. In the conflict with doubt, cast your thought wider and deeper. Do not let your thought be debased, let it transcend the conditions and the limitations of this earth.'[37]

[33] S. V. Nosovich, memoir, *MMP*. Cf. *Mochul'skii*, p. 74, where a similar remark of May 1940 is quoted.

[34] See N. Berdyaev, *The Destiny of Man* (London 1937) pp. 338–59, esp. 342. First published as *O naznachenii cheloveka* (Paris 1931). In a comment on Mother Maria's experience in Ravensbrück Berdiaev was later to write that 'she succeeded better with her Christian social work *in this hell* than she did in Paris' (MS note, *MMP*, italics mine).

[35] P. H. Vrijhof (1948) quoted (with additional comment) in E. A. Cohen, *Human Behaviour in the Concentration Camp* (London 1954), p. 197.

[36] V. F. Frankl, *Ein Psycholog erlebt das Konzentrazionslager* (Vienna 1947), p. 32.

[37] S. V. Nosovich, *VRDP*, No. 2, p. 48.

She herself practised the precept. On one occasion she made use even of the camp's crematoria to bolster a fellow prisoner's morale. A crematorium with two ovens had been installed at Ravensbrück by April 1943; a third oven was added towards the end of 1944. By that time their high chimneys (which are still preserved) ceaselessly belched out clouds of smoke, an ever-present reminder of the standard and only too accessible route out of the camp, 'up the chimney'.[38] 'When we were awakened at 4 a.m., the first thing we saw was the flaming smoke, the first thing we were aware of was the smell', wrote one of the prisoners later.[39] 'It is only here, immediately above the chimneys, that the billows of smoke are oppressive', commented Mother Maria. 'But when they rise higher they turn into light clouds before being dispersed altogether in limitless space. In the same way our souls, once they have torn themselves away from this sinful earth, move by means of an effortless unearthly flight into eternity, where there is life full of joy.'[40]

'She once calculated, in a completely calm and business-like manner, that as the result of the terrible death rate we would all be dead within five months', wrote Sophia Nosovich. ' "We'll all be up there", she said, indicating the smoke tinged with red flame of the crematorium chimney. I stupidly started to console her. She looked at me with astonishment and sorrow.'[41]

Much earlier, long before the camp, she had written:

We believe. And in accordance with the strength of our belief we sense that death ceases to be death, that it becomes birth into eternity, and that our earthly torments are transformed into birth pangs. There are times when we become so aware of the approach of the hour for this grace-endowed birth that we are prepared to say even to

[38] There were variants of this phrase, such as *durch den Kamin nach Hause* or *sortir par la cheminée*.
[39] Gemma La Guardia Gluck, *My Story* (New York 1961), p. 71.
[40] Recounted by a Ravensbrück prisoner and quoted by D. E. Skobtsov in *MM* (1947), p. 7.
[41] S. V. Nosovich, memoir, *MMP*.

our torments, 'Grow stronger, pulverize me, be unbearable, merciless and swift, because my spiritual body wishes to arise, because I wish to be born into eternity, because I already feel constricted in this sub-heavenly womb, because I want to go home to my Father and I am prepared to give up everything and to pay with any torments whatsoever for admission to my paternal and eternal home.'[42]

She was to express similar thoughts in a brief message which she asked a fellow prisoner, E. A. Novikova, to memorize and to convey – if ever that should prove possible – to Metropolitan Evlogii, Fr Sergii Bulgakov and her mother.

My state at present is such that I completely accept suffering in the knowledge that this is how things ought to be for me, and if I am to die I see in this a blessing from on high.[43]

Such an acceptance of death enhanced life. As Lucie Adelsberger was to write on the basis of her experience in both Auschwitz and Ravensbrück:

We expected death at any minute, and life which might continue for only a mere week or day or hour became extremely precious [. . .], concentrated and condensed, liberated from everything inessential and superficial. This insight into authentic life [. . .] elevated the personality, despite [. . .] our bestial way of life, to the level of the human or even above it. This sublimation was all the more pure since it was free from the fear of death. We were prepared for death, but this did not make us at all passive or dumb, but on the contrary, firm and strong. Death was close and tangible [. . .], but we were no longer afraid of it. And it is only to someone who has ceased to fear death that

---

[42] *MM* (1947), p. 132.

[43] The message was delivered in due course, although Fr Sergii Bulgakov, who died in July 1944, was not to be one of its recipients. Quoted by S. B. Pilenko, MS memoir, *MMP*; *MM* (1947), p. 152.

life belongs in all its fulness and without any limitations whatsoever.[44]

At first it seemed as if death was not necessarily imminent for Mother Maria. On 28 January 1944 a postcard from her reached Paris after a month in transit. 'I am strong and healthy', she wrote in German, and added that she was thinking of her work and of the future. None the less, after only eight months in the camp during its 'least murderous period',[45] she felt bound to add in Russian, 'I have altogether become an old woman'.[46]

However she conserved her energy as best she could. It may be that at one stage she was involved with other French prisoners in dragging a heavy iron roller about the streets of the camp for twelve hours per day.[47] Even so, the work was not necessarily as closely supervised as other assignments and it offered the occasional respite.[48] But in general she succeeded in avoiding hard labour.[49] Indeed, there were times when 'by general and tacit complicity, and without the knowledge of our guards, she remained in the block and did not work [at all].'[50] At other times she worked in the knitwear workshop where the routine was tedious and exhausting, but where the threat to life and limb was less obvious than for the work parties in the forests and marshes around the camp. In the summer of 1943 she spent some weeks in the camp infirmary: it was then possible for its inmates to gain exemption from roll calls as well as work, and it was not yet the anteroom of death which it was to become in later times.

[44] L. Adelsberger, 'Psychologische Beobachtungen im Konzentrazionslager Auschwitz', *Schweitzerische Zeitschrift für Psychologie und ihre Andwendung*, Band vi (1947), p. 129. The author arrived at Ravensbrück in January 1945.

[45] Tillion, *Ravensbrück* (1973), p. 48.

[46] Quoted in *Mochul'skii*, p. 77. Present location unknown. According to S. B. Pilenko (MS note, *MMP*) another card was received in May 1944, but there is no record of its content.

[47] A. Tveritinova in *Zvezda* (1960), No. 4, p. 131.

[48] Tillion, *Ravensbrück* (1973), p. 185.

[49] Rosane Lascroux, letter to F. T. Pianov (11 June 1945), *MMP*.

[50] Jacqueline Péry, memoir, *MMP*.

Mother Maria was assigned to block 27, at the south-west corner of the camp. But she formed a link with prisoners in barracks other than her own, particularly in block 31, where many Soviet prisoners were housed. For their part, the Russians would penetrate to her. 'As soon as some were despatched to work in the factories, others would come to take their place', noted Rosane Lascroux. 'I do not know exactly what Mother Maria would say to them, but they would go off radiant.' When they came to her in an oppressed state of mind she would comfort them and 'embrace them like children'.[51] She was on particular good terms with Gaiana's younger contemporaries, whose spirit of dedication and self-sacrifice she admired. She spoke to them about the western way of life; she discussed Russia's past history and future prospects. She also read and explained extracts from the Gospels to them. When she lay helpless in the infirmary the precious text was stolen from her.

Food was rare at the best of times. The theft of food was understandably equated with murder, and prisoners were known to punish it with death. Even the least palatable refuse was treasured. None the less Mother Maria received occasional presents which she carefully set aside for others. It was an act which required exceptional will power and altruism when even non-existent food acquired commercial value. The lack of food provoked countless dreams and conversations in which the real product was replaced by fantasy to such a degree that 'many deprived themselves of their last piece of bread so as to exchange it for a pencil stub and a scrap of paper in order to write down those delicious recipes which would anyway be thrown out as rubbish by pitiless policewomen or room cleaners at the very next search'.[52] In the words of Micheline Maurel,

Hunger affected all our feelings, even love, and little by little it began to displace them. At first I longed for a happy reunion with my husband and family [. . .]. Then I visual-

[51] Rosane Lascroux, memoir (1975), *MMP*.
[52] E. A. Novikova in *VRDP*, No. 2, p. 53.

ized my partner only with large loaves in his arms. I was afraid that my family would not have sufficient notice of my return and would not have prepared anything to eat. It was terrible to imagine my return home to my loved ones whose kitchen might be empty. Later still I no longer even imagined the people I loved, only bread. And it generally made little difference who was giving it to me.[53]

Mother Maria perceived only too well how such fantasies could degrade a person and distort relationships: 'She was angry only when people started talking of recipes or yearning for second helpings, though unfortunately we were long since incapable of discussing anything else.'[54]

Some of her food presents came from the Russians who worked in details outside the camp in the fields. Thus they were able to smuggle back the occasional carrot or potato. She hid such treasures in a box for distribution to prisoners in dire need. She made similar provision in the case of the rare food parcels which arrived from the outside world. The prisoners formed groups to share them, and she belonged to such a group. But she was also concerned to divide at least her portion with needy prisoners who did not belong. A girl known as Zouzou, who was dying of tuberculosis, was to be a regular recipient of extra food from the parcels of this group.[55] Only when Mother Maria's own health eventually declined to a disturbing degree was she forced to relent and simply to sustain herself.[56]

For as the months passed the camp routine began to leave its imprint on her. Her legs – subjected to swelling from endless roll calls in sub-zero temperatures – grew progressively weaker, and one of her fellow prisoners, Inna Webster, acted as her crutches. Even so, her vitality did not desert her. 'In the morning, that is at four o'clock, an hour before the signal for roll call, we always went together for a walk, and

[53] Micheline Maurel, *Un camp très ordinaire* (Paris 1957), p. 134. On food fantasies see pp. 134–8.
[54] E. A. Novikova in *VRDP*, No. 2, p. 59.
[55] Solange Périchon, *o.* (1964).
[56] I. N. Webster, *MM* (1947), p. 162.

she talked, told stories and dreamed dreams. Here was literally a torrent of projects and plans. Immediately on her return she would naturally go off to Les Feuillardes [. . .] and write a vast book on Ravensbrück. . . .'[57] In the event the book was never to be written. Not even the two poems which she composed on the theme of the camp were to survive it.

Only a single embroidery was to be preserved of her work, a kerchief which depicted the Normandy landings of 1944 in the style of the Bayeux tapestry.[58] Mother Maria had taken a bet that a Russian victory would precede any such landing. The work was undertaken both as a forfeit and a celebration. 'She worked it during roll calls [. . .], almost without looking and without any outline', wrote Rosane Lascroux, who commissioned the embroidery.

The material was my camp kerchief [. . .]. The colours were obtained by a Polish friend, who worked on the dyeing of SS shirts. The threads were derived from the insulation of electric flexes, which were cut and bared with the help of the camp's Siemens machinery. The needle was stolen from the [camp's] tailoring workshops of the killer and torturer Uscha Binder. Our fellow prisoners brought all these [materials] at the risk of their lives for the embroidery, this masterpiece, to be created.[59]

It was the summer of 1944.

The war was drawing to a close. The prisoners who had served a purpose in upholding German might through their labours were soon to be seen as a threat to German prestige in the event of Hitler's defeat. Consideration was now given to the destruction of the records, installations, even inmates of the camps. Thus 'towards the end [of February 1945] we received Himmler's order to prevent any concentration camp

[57] I. N. Webster, *MM* (1947), pp. 161–2.
[58] An earlier work in the same style (late 1930s) is the Life of David from Lourmel (p. 35).
[59] Rosane Lascroux, memoir (1975), *MMP*; also personal communication (1981). The embroidery remains in the possession of Rosane Lascroux (Paris). It is reproduced on plate 17.

detainees from falling into enemy hands', testified Karl Gebhardt. 'It was Kaltenbrunner who circulated the order. I
personally overheard [the] telephone discussions between
Himmler and Kaltenbrunner.'[60] Meanwhile the implementation of a parallel plan to evacuate the camps of eastern Europe
in the face of the Red Army's advance significantly increased
the population at Ravensbrück from December 1944 and led
Fritz Suhren's camp administration to consider an acceleration of the death rate even in advance of Himmler's edict.

In the words of Inna Webster,

> The last months of 1944 and the first of 1945 proved fateful
> for many, including Mother Maria. Letters and parcels
> were no longer received. The camp food, which was in any
> case atrocious, deteriorated and only half as much of it was
> distributed; hygienic and sanitary conditions became
> appalling. Instead of 800 to a block, the number rose to
> 2,500, people slept three to a bunk, lice devoured us, typhus
> and dysentery became a common scourge and decimated
> our ranks.[61]

By March 1945 Mother Maria's condition had become critical: in Jacqueline Péry's estimation, 'she had reached the
limits of human endurance'.

> She always remained lying down between roll calls, she no
> longer spoke or hardly spoke, she was absorbed in some
> endless meditation. Already she no longer belonged to the
> land of the living. Her face was striking to observe, not
> because of her ravaged features – we were accustomed to
> such a sight – but because of its intense expression of
> terrible inner suffering [. . .]. Already it bore the marks of
> death. Nevertheless Mother Maria made no complaint. She
> kept her eyes closed and seemed to be in a state of continual
> prayer. This, I think, was her garden of Gethsemane.[62]

[60] Quoted in Tillion, *Ravensbrück* (1973), p. 188.
[61] I. N. Webster, *MM* (1947), p. 162.
[62] Jacqueline Péry, memoir, *MMP*. Jacqueline Péry occupied the bunk
above Mother Maria.

Hers was not a simple and gradual decline. It resulted from a disastrous decision which she (and several thousand other prisoners) took to accept a harmless-looking pink card as a token of age, illness or fatigue. They were being freely issued in November-December 1944 with the assurance that the bearer would be excused much of the camp routine. Inna Webster was dismayed at her decision: it was common knowledge in the camp that any change was invariably for the worse. But Mother Maria was not to be dissuaded. Not only did the card bring promise of unwonted privileges, it also absolved her from contributing to the German war effort. 'You are a regular pessimist, whereas I am delighted.'[63]

Rumours were soon set in circulation concerning the newly reorganized *Jugendlager* (or Youth Camp), a kilometre to the south-east of Ravensbrück itself.[64] As Denise Dufournier recalled,

The most optimistic rumours were officially circulated as to the organization and régime of the new Youth Camp. They extolled the charming scenery, they gave assurances that roll calls would be abolished and that food would be of better quality and more abundant and that each person would be entitled to a bed. From experience we had a lively distrust of any measures taken with a view to improving our living conditions [. . .]: the sick had been poisoned on the plea of curing their insomnia [. . .]. The betting was for and against; the stakes were certainly grave.[65]

However, acceptance of the pink card meant that the die was cast. From 15 January 1945 the ill and the aged were rounded up and transferred to the Jugendlager. Mother Maria herself was taken there on 31 January in the company of other card holders, many of them already maimed by the

[63] I. N. Webster, *MM* (1947), p. 163.
[64] Formerly a camp for juvenile delinquents, hence its title. Also known as Uckermark camp.
[65] Denise Dufournier, *Ravensbrück, The Women's Camp of Death* (London 1948), pp. 120–1.

141

'medical' experiments which were formerly conducted in the camp by Karl Gebhardt and his associates.

The suspicions of the prisoners proved to be only too well founded. The Jugendlager had been established exclusively to deal with the overcrowding of the main camp. It was nothing other than a 'murderous hoax':[66] a miniature extermination camp which was to feed the newly expanded crematoria twenty-four hours per day.[67]

Roll calls took two or three times as long as in the main camp, sometimes the whole day through. The principal aim was no longer to count the living but to reduce their number.[68] The reduction of the daily bread ration from a nominal 150 grammes to something like 60, with only a half ladle of meagre rutabaga soup to supplement it, worked towards the same end. In midwinter, with snow on the ground and temperatures well below freezing point (26 degrees of frost centigrade had been recorded on Christmas Eve), blankets, coats and jackets were confiscated, eventually even shoes and stockings. No less than fifty prisoners per day therefore died from 'natural causes'. But these were modest achievements and new methods were soon to be applied. Not only were all medical supplies withdrawn from the Jugendlager's *Revier*: arrangments were made for the forcible administration of poison to the patients.[69] Selections took place daily and prisoners judged to be the least healthy were despatched by shooting and (from approximately 22 January) by gas. Initially two vans were used for killings by gas. But by 2 March 1945 Ravensbrück had acquired its own gas chambers with a daily 'capacity' of something over 150 prisoners: it was located next to the crematorium ovens, immediately outside the camp walls. Several

---

[66] Germaine Tillion, *Ravensbrück* (New York 1975), p. 74.
[67] Until December 1944 the crematoria functioned only for a matter of hours on two days a week.
[68] Evidence of the SS camp doctor, Percival Treite, at the Ravensbrück trial (Hamburg 1946), quoted in Tillion, *Ravensbrück* (1973), p. 165.
[69] Tillion, *Ravensbrück* (1973), pp. 117–18; Sylvia Salvesen, *Forgive – but do not forget* (London 1958), p. 117; E. A. Novikova, *VRDP*, No. 2, p. 58.

thousand prisoners passed through the Jugendlager, yet the barracks grew progressively more and more empty.[70]

At first, despite these conditions (or perhaps in an attempt to give them an interpretation) Mother Maria worked on yet one more embroidery. It depicted the Mother of God with a crucified Christ child in her arms. In the main camp she used to obtain thread in exchange for bread (the Normandy kerchief, as a 'public' work, was an exception): the finished product would be traded for more bread in its turn. But this image held some mysterious meaning for her. However much she was asked for it, she refused to part with it. 'On our return to Paris, I will give it away free as a present, but not here', she said. 'If I manage to complete it, it will help me to leave this place alive. If I don't manage, that means I'll die.' 'She did not manage to finish it,' stated E. A. Novikova, 'for she soon fell ill, complained of her liver and lay still for days on end [. . .]. Soon, like most of us, she caught dysentery and abstained from food, hoping that the fast would save her; she lost strength rapidly.'[71]

On the distant Paris market she had been able to obtain countless bargains to satisfy the needs of others. Here, by contrast, when she needed a mere comb to combat lice in her hair, she had to pay dearly for it: two rations of the now superfluous bread. But even though she was too weak to make more than the occasional use of the fine comb, she still retained her sense of humour. Even the sight of her own emaciated body could amuse her. 'She sometimes laughed and said, "What funny legs we have these days: thin, gangly, like little boys' legs, with just the knees protruding".' Despite everything, 'she always smiled when she spoke to someone'. And her optimism was still in evidence. When Novikova once asked her, 'What do you think, Mother, are we going to walk out of here after all?', she replied, 'While we may not walk out and will have to be carried, I am deeply convinced that we shall remain alive. I have no doubts about that.'[72]

[70] E. A. Novikova, *VRDP*, No. 2, pp. 60, 61.
[71] Ibid., p. 59.
[72] Ibid., p. 59.

Indeed, to survive in the Jugendlager for five whole weeks was in itself an achievement which seemed to augur well. At the end of this period there was an unexpected and incomprehensible transfer of prisoners back to the main camp. If this happened on 3 March, as seems likely, it would have followed immediately on other transfers from within the main camp both to the Jugendlager and, as ominously, to Mauthausen (2 March), and it may be explained by reference to them. Many of the former Jugendlager prisoners believed they had escaped death. 'It is incredible that any of us have been allowed back', said one of them to Sylvia Salvesen. '[. . .] I could never have imagined that I should ever weep with joy at returning to this camp.'[73] Mother Maria returned with them and was once more lodged in block 27.

Inna Webster located her on the following day.

I froze with horror when I saw the change in her appearance. All that was left of her was skin and bone, her eyes were festering, and she exuded that nightmarish sweet smell of those infected with dysentery [. . .]. It was the first time that she was [as] gentle and affectionate with me; she herself evidently needed tenderness and compassion.

Certainly, it was no longer merely a question of Webster acting as a physical prop. 'We won't part again', said Mother Maria. 'I shall survive. You're made of granite, you'll pull me through.' It was not for Inna Webster to challenge these assumptions. But 'I asked myself inwardly, what could this "granite" achieve?'[74]

March was a month of intensified roll calls and selections. According to the deputy commandant of the camp Johann Schwarzhüber, it was at the end of February that 'Suhren [the commandant] told us that he had received an order from Reichsführer Himmler by which all women who were ill or

[73] Sylvia Salvesen, *Forgive – but do not forget* (London 1958), p. 205.
[74] I. N. Webster, *MM* (1947), pp. 163–4.

unable to walk were to be killed'.[75] Suhren had long since anticipated such orders and was already acting in accordance with them. But their promulgation, together with the worsening war situation, prompted unprecedented acceleration of his programme.

Roll calls were in themselves difficult for Mother Maria to endure. She was fortunate in gaining the sympathy of one of the block's three superintendents, Krystyna. The latter was a woman 'in whose character all the forces of hell seemed to be concentrated'.[76] But she possessed a few favourites, of whom Mother Maria now became one. With Krystyna's consent, Mother Maria could rise only at the last minute for roll calls. Moreover she could stand behind Inna Webster and lean against her back.

The roll calls had now acquired a new dimension. Ever more frequently they provided the setting for selections, and Mother Maria was at an obvious disadvantage in respect of them. Denise Dufournier describes their procedure:

> We were drawn up in ranks of five. At a given signal, one rank moved away. When our turn came, with bare legs and nervous, rapid steps, we started off. We had to cover about fifty yards before the 'selector' who, bent double, carefully watched our legs. From time to time he would raise his hand.[77]

Or else a gesture with a whip would indicate his verdict: to the left meant death, to the right, a reprieve. Then the prisoners' numbers would be taken. Later, tarpaulin-covered vans would collect the condemned and take them to the Jugendlager or else direct to the gas chambers.

The prisoners of block 27 no longer went out to work. On the contrary, they were forbidden to leave the block. Their

---

[75] Johann Schwarzhüber, evidence at the Hamburg trial (1946), quoted in Tillion, *Ravensbrück* (1973), pp. 189–90. Evidence confirmed by F. Suhren and K. Gebhardt (ibid., loc. cit.).
[76] E. A. Novikova, *VRDP*, No. 2, p. 61.
[77] Denise Dufournier, *Ravensbrück, The Women's Camp of Death* (London 1948), p. 145.

time was spent waiting for the next roll call, the next selection, the next random raid. On one level it was possible to say that 'our only occupation was searching for lice and dreaming of extra helpings [of soup]'.[78] On another level, 'we lived in a state of nervous tension which, together with the effects of hunger, drove many out of their mind. Mother Maria remained silent and calm. Until then we had succeeded in hiding her at the critical moment from the SS.'[79] And there were many such moments that month.

After a sporadic search of the block on 23 and 29 March, three trucks took victims off to the Jugendlager. On both occasions Mother Maria (with Krystyna's support) was hidden on the so-called 'fifth floor' between roof and ceiling. At other times she was hidden beneath the bunks. 'But on Good Friday [30 March] 1945 it was impossible to use any of our tricks.'[80]

Was Mother Maria herself selected? Or did she offer herself in exchange for a fellow prisoner who had already been selected? The accounts are not at one on this issue. But this may simply be so because they refer to two different stages in the process. Two separate selections should be taken into account: the first would have taken place in the main camp on Good Friday, the other in the Jugendlager on the following day.[81]

At the same time, the question of her possible martyrdom

---

[78] E. A. Novikova, *VRDP*, No. 2, p. 61.

[79] Jacqueline Péry, memoir, *MMP*.

[80] Ibid. Good Friday by the western calendar. The Orthodox Easter that year was celebrated five weeks later.

[81] The analysis of these events is further complicated by the striking correspondence between the surviving accounts of Mother Maria's last day and that of her fellow prisoner, the Catholic nun Elisabeth Rivet, mother-superior of the Order of Notre-Dame de Compassion (Lyon). The possibility should not be excluded *a priori* that two Christians in a crowd of thousands acted in a similar fashion, in identical conditions and independently of each other. It is also possible that details from either account might have been assimilated to the other from the earliest stage. The archive of the Order at Lyons contains letters from three Ravensbrück prisoners (M.-M. Rambuteau, L. Meislenberg and E. P. Lelong) who describe the last stage of Mother Elisabeth's life. However, the accounts are given at second hand.

ought not to be considered merely in relation to these final moments. In her thought and experience martyrdom was not an isolated event. It might indeed be the culmination of a process, and yet itself a process. Her commitment 'to quench the world's sorrow with my own self' was part and parcel of it, and her death its natural outcome.

On that Good Friday, the heavy gunfire of the advancing Soviet Army could already be heard in the distance. At the very gates of the camp stood a white Ford from the International Red Cross, whose representatives were ready to negotiate the release of three hundred French prisoners. But they had not been admitted: the commandant of Ravensbrück was said to be 'occupied'. He was indeed occupied. A selection had been ordered for the afternoon and all the camp's prisoners were required on parade.

The principal selector was Johann Schwarzhüber himself.

Naturally nobody any longer had any illusions about the destination of those who were to be chosen, and Schwarzhüber knew it. He was literally beaming, brimming over with *bonhomie* and good cheer, and when my rank passed in front of him 'in fives' he leaned benevolently forward towards us and said in German, 'Just march quite calmly. . .', and then with a look of depraved complicity, 'Your heart beats, doesn't it?'[82]

There was unprecedented panic among those sent to the left, of whom there were several hundred. Some struggled, and nine escaped briefly, only to be recaptured. The anguished victims had to be tempted onto the trucks with bread. This was taken back immediately they were on board: bread could be re-used.[83]

Mother Maria had not been selected. But she saw the panic and tried to console some of the victims with assurances that

---

[82] Germaine Tillion in *Ravensbrück* (*Les cahiers du Rhône* No. 20 [65]) (Neuchâtel 1946), p. 8. She is describing the selection of two days previously; no doubt her description conforms in its essentials to the selection of Good Friday as well.

[83] Tillion, *Ravensbrück*, (1973), p. 132.

the Jugendlager did not necessarily betoken death. Despite the fact that she had herself survived its rigours her words were powerless to convince, still less to encourage them.

She must have known that a return to the Jugendlager in her own case could only mean death, even if she were not sent on to the gas chamber. Nevertheless, as if to demonstrate 'that I do not believe in the gas chamber' she stepped into the crowd of those selected and took the place of one of them. 'Thus it was', wrote two eyewitnesses, 'that Mother Maria went voluntarily to [her] martyrdom in order to help her companions to die.'[84]

Jacqueline Péry was not near her at the time of the parade and thought that she herself might have been selected because of the state of her legs.

> It is also very possible that she took the place of a frantic companion. It would have been entirely in keeping with her generous life. In any case she offered herself consciously to the holocaust [. . .], thus assisting each one of us to accept the cross [. . .]. She radiated the peace of God and communicated it to us.[85]

The vans swept the prisoners away to the Jugendlager. Many were gassed that same day. Mother Maria survived the night. But she no longer had the strength to stand. Gratuitously handicapped at the end by the forcible removal of her glasses, she was taken to the gas chamber on 31 March 1945.[86] It was the eve of Easter.

That Easter Sunday the prisoners from France were told that they should assemble on the central Lagerstrasse on the morning of the following day. Prisoners from the Jugendlager

---

[84] Two (communist) fellow prisoners, quoted in *Mochul'skii*, pp.77–8. Mochul'skii's source was an article which appeared in *Témoignage Chrétien* (summer 1945). Solange Périchon accepts that such an exchange took place, although she herself did not witness it (letter to the author, 1964).

[85] Jacqueline Péry, memoir, *MMP*.

[86] I. N. Webster (*MM* 1947, p. 165) quotes the evidence of Krystyna and another trusty (*blokowa*) who saw Mother Maria listed with those gassed on that date. But the list itself probably perished with most of the other Ravensbrück documents soon after.

were required to attend as well. The Red Cross were at last being brought into play. The release of three hundred prisoners had been agreed.

The camp administration sought to enrich the earth sloping down to the nearby lake by scattering the prisoners' ashes there, including those of Mother Maria ('O Lord, this is not I,' she had written long before, 'it is a handful of grey ash/in which are buried all desires and passions').[87] The Nazi authorities little appreciated that a life such as hers was capable of nourishing the world on quite a different plane. And they falsely equated the brutality of death with its finality.

But it was Mother Maria's conviction that 'death has lost its devastating sting'.[88] Several years later one of her friends, Georgii Raevskii, was to be reminded of this in a simple, vivid dream. He saw Mother Maria walking across a cornfield at a steady pace. He was surprised and said, 'But Mother Maria, they told me you were dead.'

She looked at me over the top of her glasses kindly, but with a hint of mischief.
'Well, no matter what they say. You can see I am alive.'[89]

[87] *Stikhi* (1949), p. 52.
[88] *Stikhi* (1949), p. 71.
[89] G. A. Raevskii, *Russkaia Mysl'*, 1 August 1961.

BIBLIOGRAPHY OF WRITINGS BY MOTHER MARIA

Minor pieces which appeared in the newspapers *Dni* (Berlin/Paris) and *Posledniia Novosti* (Paris) are not listed. Apart from the journal *Volia Rossii* (Prague), the almanack *Krug* (Berlin) and the paper *Put' zhizni* (Petsery) all émigré periodicals mentioned in the bibliography were published in Paris.

E. Kuz'mina-Karavaeva, *Skifskie cherepki* (St Petersburg, Tsekh poetov, 1912), pp. 46. Her début as a poet.
Iurali (Petrograd 1915), pp. 94. A prose poem.
Ruf' (Petrograd 1916), pp. 139+iv. A volume of short poems (with lyrical introduction).
Iurii Danilov [=E. Iu. Skobtsova], 'Ravnina russkaia', *Sovremennye zapiski*, No. 19 (1924), pp. 79–133; No. 20 (1924), pp. 125–215. An unfinished novel.
'Poslednie Rimliane', *Volia Rossii* (1924), No. 18–19, pp. 103–24. An article on the pre-Revolutionary intelligentsia.
'Klim Semenovich Baryn'kin', *Volia Rossii* (1925), No. 7–8, pp. 3–37; No. 9–10, pp. 3–38. A short story.
E. Skobtsova, *Zhatva Dukha (Zhitiia Sviatykh)* (Paris, YMCA-Press [1927], 2 vols., pp. 41 each. Stylized retelling of saints' lives.
'Sviataia zemlia', *Put'*, No. 6 (1927), pp. 95–101.
'Izuchenie Rossii', *Vestnik Russkogo Studencheskogo Khristianskogo Dvizheniia* (1927), No. 9, pp. 17–19.
A. Khomiakov (Paris, YMCA-Press, 1929), pp. 61.
Dostoevskii i sovremennost' (Paris, YMCA-Press, 1929), pp. 74.
Mirosozertsanie Vladimira Solov'eva (Paris, YMCA-Press, 1929), pp. 61.
All three booklets aim to provide a succinct introduction to the thought of the authors in question.
'V poiskakh sinteza', *Put'*, No. 16 (1929), pp. 49–68.
'K istokam', *Sovremennye zapiski*, No. 38 (1929), pp. 488–500.

'O iurodivykh', *Vestnik Russkogo Studencheskogo Khristianskogo Dvizheniia* (1930), No. 8–9, pp. 3–13.

'Rozhdenie v tvorenie', *Put'*, No. 30 (1931), pp. 35–47.

'Sotsial'nye sdvigi v emigratsii', *Novyi Grad*, No. 2 (1932), pp. 70–4.

Monakhinia Mariia (Skobtsova), 'Sotsial'nyi vopros i sotsial'naia real'nost', *Novyi Grad*, No. 4 (1932), pp. 73–6.

'K delu', *Novyi Grad*, No. 5 (1932), pp. 93–8.

'Krest i serp s molotom', *Novyi Grad*, No. 6 (1933), pp. 78–81.

Monakhinia Mariia, 'Istoki tvorchestva', *Put'*, No. 43 (1934), pp. 35–48.

'Pravoslavnoe Delo', *Novyi Grad*, No. 10 (1935), pp. 111–15.

'U groba ottsa Aleksandra' and 'Otets Aleksandr kak dukhovnik' in the symposium *Pamiati o. Aleksandra Elchaninova* (Paris 1935), pp. 21–4, 56–9. The first article signed M.M.

'Vstrechi s Blokom. (K piatnadtsatiletiiu so dnia smerti', *Sovremennye zapiski*, No. 62 (1936), pp. 211–28. Republished, with introduction by D. E. Maksimov, in *Uchenye zapiski Tartuskogo gosudarstvennogo universiteta*, vyp. 209 (1968), pp. 265–78. The republication is under the name E. Iu. Kuz'mina-Karavaeva.

'Mistika chelovekoobshcheniia', *Krug. Al'manakh*, No. 1 [1936], pp. 152–9.

Stikhi (Berlin, Petropolis [1937]), pp. 97+7. The only collection of verse of her maturity published in her lifetime. Her own copy, which she illustrated with forty-eight pen and ink drawings, is preserved in *MMP*.

'Ispytanie svobodoi', *Vestnik. Organ tserkovno-obshchestvennoi zhizni* (1937), No. 1–2, pp. 11–15. In the same number an anonymous note by her on Orthodox Action (pp. 24–6). The journal is a continuation of *Vestnik Russkogo Studencheskogo Khristianskogo Dvizheniia* (to which name it was soon to revert).

'Pis'mo v redaktsiiu', *Vestnik. Organ tserkovno-obshchestvennoi zhizni* (1937), No. 3–4, pp. 24–6.

'Pod znamenem nashego vremeni', *Novyi Grad*, No. 12 (1937), pp. 115–22.

'Pod znakom gibeli', *Novyi Grad*, No. 13 (1938), pp. 145–52. Reprinted in *MM* (1947), pp. 113–23.

'Rasizm i religiia', *Russkie zapiski* (1938), No. 11, pp. 150–7.

'Opravdanie fariseistva', *Put'*, No. 56 (1938), pp. 37–46.

'O podrazhanii Bogomateri', *Put'*, No. 59 (1939), pp. 19–30.

'Chetyre portreta', *Novyi Grad*, No. 14 (1939), pp. 26–40.

'Vtoraia zapoved' ' and 'Na strazhe svobody' in *Pravoslavnoe Delo. Sbornik I* (Paris 1939), pp. 27–44, 84–95. The anonymous preface (pp. 5–8) was also her work. 'Vtoraia zapoved' ' was reprinted in *MM* (1947), pp. 93–134.

POSTHUMOUS PUBLICATIONS

Mat' Mariia: stikhotvoreniia, poemy, misterii, vospominaniia ob areste i lagere v Ravensbriuke (Paris, La presse française et étrangère/ Oreste Zeluck, 1947), pp. 167. Contains only six pages of shorter poems, and concentrates on longer poems such as 'Pokhvala trudu' and 'Dukhov Den' ' (pp. 19–37), as well as on plays (or 'mysteries') like 'Anna' and 'Soldaty' (pp. 73–92). It also includes four articles, two of them published for the first time: 'Rozhdenie v smerti' (pp. 123–34), and 'Prozrenie v voine' (pp. 134–48). Foreword by D. E. Skobtsov (pp. 7–8). Memoirs by D. E. Skobtsov, S. B. Pilenko and I. N. Webster (pp. 151–65).

Mat' Mariia, *Stikhi* (Paris, Izdanie obshchestva druzei materi Marii, 1949), pp. 99+2. A more comprehensive and judicious selection of verse. The greater part of the book is devoted to short poems (pp. 15–74). In addition there is one 'mystery', 'Sem' chash' (pp. 76–99); also an introduction by S. B. Pilenko (pp. 5–11) and a note on Mother Maria's poetry by the editor, G. A. Raevskii (pp. 13–14).

POEMS PUBLISHED SEPARATELY IN THE AUTHOR'S LIFETIME

Rukonog. Sbornik stikhov i kritiki (Moscow, Tsentrifuga, 1914).

E. Kuz'mina-Karavaeva (three poems).

Vesennii salon poetov (Moscow, Zerna, 1918).

E. Kuz'mina-Karavaeva (three poems).

Sovremennye zapiski, No. 39 (1929), pp. 170–3.

E. Kuz'mina-Karavaeva (four poems).

Sovremennye zapiski, No. 62 (1936), pp. 185–7.

Monakhinia Mariia (three poems).

Iakor'. Antologiia zarubezhnoi poezii, ed. G. Adamovich and M. Kantor

(Berlin, Petropolis, 1936), pp. 75–6. Monakhinia Mariia (two poems).

Put' zhizni, 24 July 1937. Monakhinia Mariia (one poem).

Russkie zapiski (1938), No. 3, pp. 161–4. Monakhinia Mariia (four poems).

POSTHUMOUS PUBLICATION OF INDIVIDUAL POEMS

A number of anthologies of émigré poetry contain previously published items. Hitherto unpublished poems are to be found in Hackel, *MM* (1980), pp. 22–3, 48, 78–9, 87, 88, 142, 149, 151, 160, 163.

INDEX

References to Mother Maria are dispersed throughout the index. She is designated as MM, regardless of whether she bore her maiden, married or monastic name at the time. With few exceptions, notes are not indexed.

Adelsberger, Lucie 135–6
Akhmatova, Anna Andreevna
    (1889–1966) 80
Anapa, MM acting mayor of 9,
    90–2, 94
    MM cultivates land at 88–9
    mentioned 76, 93–5
Anderson, Paul B. (Pavel
    Frantsovich) (*b.* 1894) 66
Anna, mystery play by MM 47–9
antisemitism, Nazi policy of 47–9,
    106–15, 120, 122–3
arrest of MM, in 1918 93
    in 1943 94–5, 120–2
Auschwitz extermination camp
    107, 114, 117n, 133, 135

Bakhst, Fr Valentin 52
baptism certificates, Fr Dimitrii
    Klepinin issues equivalent of
    111–12, 117
    Nazi legislation creates need for
    111
Basil the Blessed, Saint (1464–
    1552) 71
Berdiaev, Nikolai Aleksandrovich
    (1874–1948) 30, 34, 45, 65, 69,
    71, 79, 115, 133
Bestuzhev Courses for Women (St
    Petersburg) 80
Blok, Aleksandr Aleksandrovich
    (1880–1921) 82–6, 88–9

Bolshevik rule, MM's attitude to
    90–3
Bolshevik (Social-Democrat) Party
    78–9
Buchenwald concentration camp
    126–7
Budzinskii, Dr (mayor of Anapa)
    93–4
Bulgakov, Archpriest Sergii (1871–
    1944) 17–18, 34, 39, 65–6, 69,
    100, 135, *pl.* 6
Bussy-en-Othe, Orthodox convent
    at 47n

'Captain Glan', father of Gaiana
    85
certificates of baptism *see* baptism
    certificates
Chamberlain, Houston Stewart
    (1855–1927) 108n
chapels founded by MM, at Noisy-
    le-Grand 62
    at rue de Lourmel 35, 41–2, 101,
    119, 129
    at villa de Saxe 34, 41–2
character of MM *see* personality of
    MM
Chertkov, Fr Mikhail (1878–1945)
    62, 66
Christianity and Judaism 108,
    113–14, 120, 122

civil war, Russian 1–2, 57, 92–4
Compiègne, detention camp at
    104, 106, 124–6
concentration camps *see* name of
    individual camps
Confessing Church (Germany)
    120n
Constantinople 2–3
convents and monasteries in USSR
    23, 43
Courtin, Mother Dorofeia 41, 46n
crematoria at Ravensbrück 97,
    134, 142, 149

deaconess *manquée?*, MM as 71
deaconesses, move to restore
    (Orthodox) order of 71
death, MM's attitude to 5–6, 16,
    51, 76, 98–9, 101–2, 129,
    134–5, 140, 148–9
    MM's forebodings of 95–7
Deutsche Christen 108
divorce, Byzantine legislation on
    19
    MM and 2, 17, 19, 84, 96
Dora concentration camp 127–8
Drancy 106–7, 114
drug addicts, MM's concern for
    12, 54
Dufournier, Denise 141, 145

Easter celebrated at Lourmel
    (1940) 101
Eichmann, Karl Adolf (1902–62)
    112
Elizaveta Medvedeva, Mother *see*
    Medvedeva, Sophia
    Veniaminovna
embroidery by MM 35, 139, 143,
    pl. 15–17
emigration, the Russian (post-
    Revolutionary), church life in
    18, 22, 41, 43–4, 72–3
    economic plight of 1–2, 10–12,
    51–3, 56–7
    Europe first encounters 1–2
    French legislation concerning
    30–1, 56–7, 60, 63
    Orthodox Action and 67
    war-time attitudes of 74, 102–3,

107–9, 121–2, 126
    see also tuberculosis, Russian
    emigration seeks to combat
Evdokia Meshcherakova, Mother
    (1895–1977) 41–4, 47, 120,
    pl. 9
Evlogii Georgievskii, Metropolitan
    (1866–1946) *pl.* 5, 6
    appoints clergy to Lourmel 41,
    44, 100
    approves divorce of MM 19
    expects MM to develop
    conventual life 22, 41
    disappointed 26–7
    furthers cause of TB patients
    61–3
    personality 18, 70
    president of Orthodox Action 66
    professes MM 26–7
    valued by MM 23, 31–2
    withdraws personnel from
    Lourmel 47
    mentioned 17, 44, 71, 135

Fedotov, Georgii Petrovich (1886–
    1951) 45, 65, 69, 106, 119n,
    pl. 13
Félix Faure, rue de 36
'Final Solution of the Jewish
    Problem' 109
Folly for Christ's sake, MM
    favours 26, 32, 47, 71, 73–4
Fondaminskaia, Amalia Osipovna
    (*d.* 1935) 105
Fondaminskii, Ilia Isidorovich
    [Bunakov-] (1880–1942) 45,
    69, 99, 103–7
Fools for Christ's sake 25–6, 71
François Gérard, rue 35, 108
Frank, Semen Liudvigovich (1877–
    1950) 69
Frere, Walter, Bishop of Truro
    (1863–1938) 47

Gaiana Kuz'mina-Karavaeva
    (1913–36), daughter of MM
    born 85
    departs for USSR 6–7, 38, 41
    dies 7

mentioned 2, 8–9, 54, 62, 75, 129

gas chambers at Ravensbrück 142, 145, 148

Gavronskaia (aided by Iura Skobtsov) 117

Gebhardt, Karl (1898–1948) 139–40, 142

Gestapo headquarters (Paris) 118–19, 121, 123

Gillet, Archimandrite Lev (1893–1980) 7, 18, 41, 52, 64–5, 71, 97n, 105, 114n

Gippius, Vasilii Vasil'evich (1890–1942) 83

'going to the people' considered by MM 75, 82–5, 89, 99

Gumilev, Nikolai Stepanovich (1886–1921) 80

hell, perpetuity doubted of 132–3

Himmler, Heinrich (1900–45) 110, 114, 139–40, 144

Hofmann, Hans 117–22

hospitals, La Rochefoucauld (Paris) 61
    Pasteur Institute (Paris) 4
    St Slie (Jura) 57–60
    Val-de-Grâce (Paris) 107

hostages, Nazi policy in respect of 104, 118

Iafimovich, Elizaveta Aleksandrovna (1818–1906) 77

image of God in man, MM perceives 13, 43, 51–2, 68

Isaac of Syria, Saint (7th century) 54–5

Iura (Iurii Danilovich) Skobtsov (1920–44), son of MM
    arrested 117–18
    imprisoned 123–8
    meets MM at Compiègne 124
    mentioned 2, 41, 115, 120

Ivanov, Viacheslav Ivanovich (1886–1949) 79, 82

'Jew', Nazi definition of 110–11

John Cassian, Saint (c. 360–435) 28

Judaism and Christianity 108, 113–14, 120, 122

Jugendlager, Ravensbrück annexe 141–6, 148
    MM inmate of 141, 143–4

Justinian, Emperor (527–65) 19

Kaltenbrunner, Ernst (1903–46) 140

Kazachkin, Iurii Pavlovich (1899–1968) 121, 127–8

Kerensky, Aleksandr Fedorovich (1881–1970) 14, 105

Kern, Archimandrite Kiprian see Kiprian Kern, Archimandrite

Khomiakov, Aleksei Stepanovich (1804–60), MM discusses 68n

Kiprian Kern, Archimandrite (1889–1960) 44–7, 100

Klepinin, Fr Dimitrii (1900–44) pl. 13, 14
    celebrates Easter (1940) 101
    certifies church 'membership' of Jews 111–12
    establishes chapel of St Philip 119
    imprisoned 124–8
    interrogated 120
    personality 100–1, 111, 123
    mentioned 104, 107, 115, 117

Klepinina, Tamara Fedorovna (b. 1897) 121, 128

Kliachkina, Romana Semenovna 104

Krivoshein, Igor' Aleksandrovich (b. 1899) 104, 115–16, 148n

Krug, Fr Grigorii (1909–69) 62n

Krupskaia, Nadezhda Konstantinovna (1869–1939) 92

Krystyna (block superintendent at Ravensbrück) 145–6, 148n

Kuban government and rada 3, 9, 93

Kullmann, Gustav Gustavovich (1894–1961) 67

Kuz'min-Karavaev, Dmitrii Vladimirovich (1885–1959), first husband of MM 79, 84–5

Lafont, Louis Ernest (1879–1946)
  62–3
Lascroux, Rosane (*b.* 1911) 131,
  137, 139
Lenin, Vladimir Il'ich (1870–1924)
  17
Les Halles (Paris) frequented by
  MM 37–8, 52, 103, 143
Lourmel, 77 rue de *pl.* 7
  canteen at 37, 42, 45, 52, 103,
    117
  care of needy at 36–7, 39, 45, 54,
    56–7, 62, 103
  chapels at 35, 41–2, 66, 71, 101,
    119, 129
  foundation of 34–6
  lectures at 69, 72
  monastic group at 41–7
  MM considers flight from 46
  Orthodox Action founded at 66
  Resistance activities at 104,
    116–17
  support for Jews and others at
    111–12, 115–16, 121
  mentioned 50, 59, 100, 108,
    120–1, 123

Mandel'shtam, Osip Emil'evich
  (1892–1938) 80, 83
Manukhina, Tatiana Ivanovna
  (1885–1962) 27, 34, 38
Maritain, Jacques (1882–1973)
  113n
marriage of MM, to D. V.
  Kuz'min-Karavaev (1910) 84
  to D. E. Skobtsov (1919) 9, 94
martyrdom of MM? 146–8
Maurel, Micheline 137–8
Mauthausen concentration camp
  144
Medvedeva, Sophia Veniaminovna
  [= Mother Elizaveta
  Medvedeva] (1890–1974) 54,
  104, 118–20
mental hospitals investigated by
  MM 57–60
Meshcherakova, Mother Evdokia
  see Evdokia Meshcherakova,
  Mother
Metropolitan Evlogii Georgievskii

see Evlogii Georgievskii,
  Metropolitan
mobilization, MM compares
  Christian commitment to 74
Mochul'skii, Konstantin
  Vasil'evich (1892–1948) *pl.* 13
  befriends Iura Skobtsov 118
  befriends MM 22n, 33–4
  collaborates with MM 45, 64–6,
    69
  quoted/mentioned 22, 29–30,
    34–5, 38–9, 43, 46, 51, 75,
    91–101, 109, 113, 115
Moisenay-le-Grand, Orthodox
  convent at 47, 120
monasteries and convents in USSR
  23, 43
monastic profession by MM 19–21,
  24
  assessed by others 22, 26–7, 30,
    70–1
monasticism, renewal of, MM
  urges 25–7, 48–9
  social service integral to, MM
  insists 26–7, 29–30
  traditional forms of, MM
  criticizes 23–5, 27, 48–9
Moscow 7n, 17–18, 62, 75, 89,
  92–3
Moshkovskaia, Iulia Iakovlevna 84

Nastia (Anastasia Danilovna)
  Skobtsova (1922–6), daughter
  of MM 2–4, 8–9, 15–16, 19,
  129, *pl.* 3, 4
Nazi attitudes scorned by MM 99,
  107–8, 119
Nechaev, Archimandrite Afanasii
  (*d.* 1943) 111n
Nicholas of Myra, Saint (4th
  century) 28
Noisy-le-Grand, MM's foundation
  at 36, 53, 55–6, 61–3, 115–18
Nosovich, Sophia V. 132–4
Novikova, E. A. 135, 143
Novorossiisk, MM's departure
  from 2–3

Obolenskaia, Mother Blandina 41,
  46n

Orthodox Action (*Pravoslavnoe Delo*), financed 66–7, 119
founded (1935) 65–6
principles 65–8, 108, 126
prohibited (1943) 123
Russian emigration served by 67
mentioned 104–5, 117
Ottsup [=Raevskii], Georgii Andreevich (1897–1963) 115n, 149

Périchon, Solange 130–1, 148n
personality of MM 7–8, 30, 34–5, 40, 46, 50–1, 70, 108–9, 122, 129–33, 143, 149
Péry, Jacqueline 131–2, 140, 148
Peters, Pastor 108, 126
Philip, Metropolitan of Moscow, Saint (1507–69) 119
Pianov, Fedor Timofeevich (1889–1969) *pl.* 10
as administrator 55–7, 61, 66, 103
arrested 121
imprisoned 103, 106, 124–7
interrogated 122
personality 55
mentioned 30, 62, 64, 71, 105, 108, 116–18
Piast, Vladimir Alekseevich (1886–1940) 83
Pilenko, Dmitrii Iur'evich (1893–1920), brother of MM *pl.* 2, 122
Pilenko, Iurii Dmitrievich (1857–1906), father of MM 76–7
Pilenko, Sophia Borisovna (1862–1962), mother of MM 2, 32n, 34, 41, 63, 75, 97, 100, 117, 121–2, 135, *pl.* 2, 13
Piukhtitsa, Orthodox convent at 23
Piux XI, Pope (1857–1939) 113
Pobedonostsev, Konstantin Petrovich (1827–1907) 76–8
poetry by MM *pl.* 11
composed 21, 109, 139
published 7, 9–10, 80n, 86, 150–3
quoted 6, 13–16, 19, 24, 32–3,

46, 48, 50–2, 95–8, 100, 113, 149
Poets' Guild (*Tsekh poetov*) 80
Pravoslavnoe Delo see Orthodox Action
Priestley, Stuart 44n, 47
Protapov (chairman of soviet, Anapa) 90–2
Pyrenean mines, MM visits 11–12

Raevskii [=Ottsup], Georgii Andreevich (1897–1963) 115n, 149
Ratner, Evgenia (*d.* 1932) 92–3
Ravensbrück concentration camp, arrival of MM at 129–30
brutalization of inmates at 130–3, 135–8
death rate accelerated at 139–40, 142–5, 147–8
group loyalties prevail at 130, 138
last days of MM at 140–9
prisoners at, MM's concern for 130–4, 137–8, 147–8
mentioned 49, 97, 99
see also crematoria; gas chambers; Jugendlager; Red Cross; 'selections'
Red Cross, arrival at Ravensbrück of 147, 149
Reitlinger, Gerald (*b.* 1900) 114
Reitlinger, Sister Ioanna 35
Resistance, French 109, 116–17
Revolution of 1905, MM's attitude to 76–9, 81
Riga (birthplace of MM), Trinity convent at 23
Rivet, Mother Elisabeth (1890–1945) 146n
Romainville prison 123–4
RSKhD *see* Russian Student Christian Movement
Ruf' (1916), preface quoted 87
Russia, MM's concern for 43, 75, 86, 98–9, 100, 131
Russian Student Christian Movement (RSKhD) *pl.* 6
aims and activities 10, 64
N.A. Berdiaev's rift with 69

Fr Lev Gillet's appeal to 64–5
staff members of: Fr Dimitrii
Klepinin 100, MM 10–12, 23,
65, F. T. Pianov 55

St Petersburg 11, 76, 84, 86
St Petersburg Theological
Academy, MM seeks to study
at 80n
St Sergius Theological Institute
(Paris) 17–19, 47
Ste Geneviève-des-Bois, Russian
cemetery at 16
Salvesen, Sylvia 114
Saussaies, rue de see Gestapo
headquarters (Paris)
schools established by MM 52
Schwarzhüber, Johann (1904–47)
144, 147
'selections' at Ravensbrück 142,
144–8
self-sacrifice, MM's acceptance of
6, 13–16, 20–1, 24, 26–7,
39–40, 47–9, 55, 74, 79, 87,
95–7, 118, 147–8
Sellier, Henri Charles (1883–1943)
63n
Skobtsov, Daniil Ermolaevich
(1884–1968), second husband
of MM 2–3, 9, 19, 36, 94, 118,
123
Skobtsov, Iura see Iura (Iurii
Danilovich) Skobtsov
Skobtsova, Nastia see Nastia
(Anastasia Danilovna)
Skobtsova
Social-Democrat (Bolshevik) Party
78–9
Socialist-Revolutionary (S–R)
Party 78–9, 89–90, 105
MM member of 89, 92–3
Solomianskaia, Mother Feodosia
46n
Star of David (Zionsstern) 112–14
Stepun, Fedor Avgustovich (1884–
1966) 45n
Stern [=Shtern], Sergei
Fedorovich (d. 1946) 104
Student Christian Movement,

Russian see Russian Student
Christian Movement
Suhren, Fritz (1908–50) 140, 145,
147

Tagore, Rabindranath (1861–1941)
28–9, 42
Tblisi 2–3
Tillion, Germaine Marie Rosine
(b. 1907) 147
Tolstoi, Aleksei Nikolaevich (1883–
1945) 6
Tower, the (Viacheslav Ivanov's
flat) 79–82
Trotsky, Lev Davidovich (1879–
1940), MM would-be assassin
of? 90
tuberculosis, Russian emigration
seeks to combat 60–3

Ugrimov, Aleksandr
Aleksandrovich 116

Vélodrome d'Hiver (Paris)
114–15, 129
Verevkina, N. 116, pl. 15
villa de Saxe 31–4, 41, 54, 69
Viskovskii, Anatolii Vasil'evich
(d. 1945) 57, 121, 127n, 128
Volunteer Army (White) 2, 93
Vrasskii, Protopresbyter Andrei
(d. 1944) 128
Vysheslavtsev, Boris Petrovich
(1877–1954) 69

Webster [=Vebster], Inna N. 138,
140–1, 144–5
Widdrington, Canon Percy
Elbrough Tinling (1879–1959)
12, 66

Zambrzhitskii, Archpriest
Konstantin (d. 1950) 106
Zander, Lev Aleksandrovich
(1893–1964) 22
Zander, Valentina Aleksandrovna
(b. 1894) 22
Zherebkov, Iurii S. 107, 109, 120
'Zouzou' (Ravensbrück prisoner)
138

699444